DEVELOPMENT OF CREATIVITY IN FAMILY

FREEDOM AND SOCIO-ECONOMIC STATUS ASPECTS

DEVELOPMENT OF CREATIVITY IN FAMILY

FREEDOM AND SOCIO-ECONOMIC STATUS ASPECTS

Dr. Ashis Kumar Debnath

Development of Creativity in Family:
Freedom and Socio-Economic Status Aspects

First Published 2021

ISBN 978-81-949754-7-2

Published by:
CRESCENT PUBLISHING CORPORATION
4806/24, Mathur Lane,
Ansari Road, Darya Ganj,
New Delhi - 110 002
Ph.: 011 - 23244131
Mob.: + 91 - 9711991838, 9999021668
E-mail: crescentbook@gmail.com
Website: www.crescentpublishingcorp.weebly.com

Typesetting by
Priyanka Graphics
New Delhi

Printed at:
Balaji Offset
Delhi

Printed in India

Dedicated to

My elder sister,

Dr. Tapati Debnath (Double Ph. D.),

A positive Reinforcer in my life.

PREFACE

Resonance is occurred only when the frequencies of the two objects are matched to each other. That is, when the periodical external force will strike the object at its particular frequency, the object will be vibrated with its maximum amplitude and energy. Similarly, the particular stimuli of the environment elicit a great response or expression within the individual, only when the stimuli are suitable for the particular field of creativity. Many research studies demand that every child has creative potential more or less, but the types of the field area of creativity are different. To identify the types of the creative potential in the child is very much essential before selecting the appropriate stimulating environment. There are so many factors associated with the development of creative potential. A few of them seem to be very essential regardless the types of creativity field. These factors of the environments directly or indirectly help in nurturing and developing creative potential in the child.

Some parents wish to nurture creativity in their children, but their efforts go in the wrong way. They are more conscious about the child's knowledge, rather than divergent thinking. In the present social perspective, they have belief in memory and knowledge and have less confidence on the creative potential of their children or they don't know how to maintain the quality in their children. However, a minimum opportunity should be given to every child in his / her early stage of life for unfolding creative potential. Because, a creative person alone can bring about an enormous change in the society. Thus, a creative person is a valuable asset to any nation.

Family is the first and basic environment to every child, where the child may get the required stimuli for his creativity development. This environment of the family again depends on some aspects which control the whole socio-emotional climate of the family as well as the development of creativity in the child. Research findings regarding these factors of creativity may draw attention of the parents and the society, so that, they can create an ideal stimulating family environment for nurturing and developing such type of valuable qualities or at least not for suppressing them.

The book consists of six chapters. The first chapter deals with the problem and its justification. The second chapter contains review of the related literature of the study. Methodology of the study, description of the tools used and the general procedure have been elaborately mentioned in the third chapter. In the fourth chapter, organization of data, descriptive statistics, graphical representation, inferential and correlational techniques and regression analysis have been described. The findings of the study and discussions on them have been consciously mentioned in the fifth chapter. At last, the sixth chapter encompasses the principal findings, conclusion and implications of the present study.

CONTENTS

LIST OF TABLES

List of Graphs

1

CONCEPTUAL BACKGROUND

1.1 Introduction

Mental abilities are distributed normally according to the law of Nature. Hence, a portion of the total population should be of superior quality and naturally some are backward in mental abilities. These backward people like mentally retarded, physically handicapped, emotionally disturbed, are easily seen in the society. But the people of superior quality, that is, talented and creative persons are almost invisible in the society of developing countries like India. Because, disability expresses itself but talent and creativity need something special for expressing themselves. Without that condition, stimulating environment, the talented and creative persons cannot unfold their abilities and as a result they become common people of the society. This is a great loss to any nation.

In order to develop a society as well as a country, the importance of knowledge and skills cannot be denied, but knowledge alone is not enough in this fast changing world. Creativity takes important roles in this case. Creativity provides the fundamental intellectual materials - ideas, concepts, insights and discovery that in course of time results in development of new theories, approaches, tools, products and a kind of mutual sharing that underline innovation. Socially transmitted creative discovery brings innovation. The highly creative persons may bring about revolutionary change in the society in the dimension of advancement. Now the question is that, who are creative?

Many research findings have established the truth that every child has creative potential more or less (Murphy, 1947; Fliegler, 1961). But the levels of creativity and the styles of creativity are different in different children.

Creative potential may be developed in a stimulating environment which is basically democratic, free and open. Torrance (1970) and Arieti (1976) emphasized the influence of culture and environment on the development of creativity. Society have been cruelled in developing creative thinking in children. Our society is so orthodox that we are not ready for any change. Any new thinking is curbed before it is expressed. Many people strongly believe that whatever exists today, is final and unchangeable. The vested interests in the society always oppose any type of contemplated change. We have always been making fun of those people who are different from ordinary people.

One of the most justifiable charge that can be labelled against our educational system is that it has neglected and all too often suppressed, the natural creativity of the young (Kneller, 1965). Education in our society is almost systematized and routinized at all levels from primary to the university. It has encouraged and has been encouraging listless passivity and rote memory. It is generally seen that our school programmes are not giving due place to the educational experience and proper environment which are conducive to the development of creative potential.

Ebel (1969) quotes Bloom and maintains that: "There is reason to believe that educational system can reduce originality and creativity. This negative effect on creativity is most marked when examinations, instructional materials and processes, all emphasize learning by rote and the goal is centred on getting through examination" [Gupta,2006].

Among three different types of environment, namely; family, social and school environment, the family environment has important roles in nurturing and fostering creativity of the children. But some parents, while wishing to foster creativity, go about it, the wrong way. They are more concerned with external success and popularity instead of with inner growth and creative potential of their children.

The family environment directly or indirectly is controlled by its components like family structure, socio-economic status, family tension, life style of the family members, professions of the members, interpersonal relationship among the members, anxiety of the family members etc. Depending upon these components a variety of environments exist in different families of the society. As an active member of the family, the child must be affected by the family environment. But the degree of influences of all components is not same on creativity in the children.

1.2 Concept of Creativity

Creativity is regarded as the ability which could bring something new into being. Again, creativity is considered only as the psychological process or processes by which novel or variable new products are created. Barron (1969) indicates that the role of creativity in the whole process of socialization is critical. A creative person can bring a revolutionary change in this world if he gets the proper environment or supporting elements to do so. Creativity has been known as a precious source of emergence, development and survival of human's culture through ages.

Creativity is recognized as a multivariate phenomenon. The different perspectives that have been adopted to study creativity and different relationships exist among them. There are indefinite numbers of ways to be creative. Therefore, the investigator who attempts to conduct research in this Masonic field faces difficulty in defining creativity.

According to Drevdahl (1956), "Creativity is the capacity of a person to produce compositions, products or ideas which are essentially new or novel and previously unknown to the producer". Here, the concept of creativity indicates the human's ability to produce new one which is original. In the same way De Bono (1993) defines as "Being creative means to bring into being something that was not there before". Spearman (1931) defines creativity as the power of the human mind to create new contents by transforming relations and thereby generating new correlates.

Guilford (1959) defines the creativity as the trait of human beings. He describes, "Creative children have a more general trait that includes not only originality, but flexibility, fluency and motivational and temperamental traits as well". Again, Wilson, Guilford and Christensen (1974) mention, "The creative process is any process by which something new is produced – an idea or an object including a new form or arrangement of old elements. The new creation must contribute to the solution of some problems". Torrance (1977) defines creativity, "as a process of becoming sensitive to problems, deficiencies, gaps of knowledge, missing elements, disharmonies and so on, identifying the difficulties, searching for solutions, making guesses or formulating hypotheses about the deficiencies, testing and retesting hypotheses and possibly modifying and retesting them and finally communicating results". According to Berk (2002), "Creativity is the ability to produce work that is original, but still appropriate and useful". Berk emphasizes rightly on the usefulness of new creation on the social context.

Guilford (1956) demonstrates "divergent thinking" as one of the most important intellectual operations by which the product or end result in the thinking process is reached. Guilford defines "divergent thinking" as a kind of mental operation in which we think in different directions, sometimes searching, sometimes seeking variety. The unique feature of divergent production is that a variety of responses is produced. He relates divergent thinking to certain well-known output. These three factors are fluency, flexibility and originality, each of which shows itself in particular forms according to the contents and products with which it is concerned.

In general, four approaches (4Ps) are used to understand the concept of creativity, namely; ***Product, Process, Person*** and the ***Press*** (the environment in which the creation comes about).

All these definitions of creativity point out that creativity as the capacity or ability of an individual to create, discover or produce a new or novel idea or object, new solutions of the problems by rearranging or reshaping the environments. A creative person is very much aware of the environment and much sensitive to the problems. His thinking is fluent, dynamic, flexible, original and novel.

1.3 Nature of Creativity

Creativity is universal quality and is not bound by the barriers of age, caste, location or culture. Every one of us possesses and is capable of demonstrating creativity to some degree in any particular field of activity. Creativity is innate as well as acquired ability of human beings. Many research findings have suggested that creativity is natural entity but there is no denial of the fact that cultural background, education, environment and experience nurtures creativity.

Creativity is more important now than ever before. This is because, creativity is a useful and effective response to evolutionary changes. Creativity is usually tied to original behaviour, and indeed, originality is necessary for creativity, but it is not sufficient. Creativity is a syndrome or complex (Albert & Runco, 1989; Mackinnon, 1983; Mumford & Gustafson, 1988), and flexibility is an important part of it. Flexibility is such characteristic feature of a creative person which enable them to cope up with the changing environments.

Creativity is not, however, just a concern and target for individuals. Its benefits are just as clear for society and culture (Simonton, 1991). Creativity plays an important role in technological advance, in the social and behavioural sciences, and in the humanities and arts (Dudek, 2003). Because of its role in innovation and entrepreneurship, creativity has become one of the key concerns of organizations and businesses [Runco, 2004].

Creativity is a departure from the stereotyped, rigid and closed thinking. It encourages and demands complete freedom to accept and express the multiplicity of responses, choices and lines of actions. It is a kind of adventurous thinking, calling a person to come out in the open to express himself according to his will and to function unrestricted by routine or previous practice.

Creativity and intelligence do not necessarily go hand-in-hand. Research findings have demonstrated that the intelligence and creativity have only a low correlation (Ebel *et al.*, 1969). It is not that one is the necessary or essential pre-requisite of the other. But a minimum level of intelligence is a necessary precondition for successful creative expression. This is of course on the assumption that there is a cut-off score of I. Q. around the normality above which aforesaid relationship holds good (Deshmukh, 1977). After presenting a thorough review of literature Torrance (1967) summarizes the correlational information about creativity and intelligence relationship as revealed in various studies. He found that the relationship between creativity and intelligence is low. It shows that it is not necessary for a highly creative person to have high intelligence. Again, the person with low intelligence may almost be high creative. On the other hand, a highly intelligent person may not be highly creative.

Similarly, there is no significant correlation between an individual's creative talent and his achievement in the school. One may be creative but score quite low on achievement tests and a topper in school may show little or no creative output.

Creativity requires creative individual to be more sensitive to the demands of a problem than the evaluation of his social environment. The creative individual is more inner-than outer orientated. He/she naturally utilizes his/her energy and potential more for the fulfilment or we can say the satisfaction of his/her creative urge than to care for the easy and pleasant security of positive peer approval. It is for this reason that the creative individuals are not very sociable [Mangal, 2005].

Some indicators of creativity belong to both intellectual as well as non-intellectual categories. These indicators are necessary to identify the creative persons. The indicators of creativity are as follows:

- **Sensitivity and awareness:** As compared to others, the creative person is more open and sensitive to his environment. Many things that strike him are missed by others. However, his interests may gradually be limiting to a few selected fields as he grows older. He shows curiosity about events, ideas and actions taking place in his surrounding environments.
- **Fluency:** The creative child is usually fluent in ideas, whether the medium of his expression is verbal or non-verbal. Such a child produces many more ideas on a question or a problem than the ordinary students of his age or class.
- **Flexibility:** The creative child is a flexible thinker. He can think of many unusual uses of a thing that most children may not think. He is also to make use of a variety of approaches to solve a particular problem.
- **Originality:** This is the most important indicator of creativity. It includes such abilities as the capacity to produce unusual ideas, solve unusual problems in unusual ways and use things or situations in an unusual manner. His suggestions are novel as well as useful.
- **Elaboration:** Another indicator of creative potential is the ability to go into details. A creative child can describe a problem in details.
- **Curiosity:** The creative child has unending curiosity about the matter, its existence, causes and consequences. A creative child is always seeking information and he is a keen observer.
- **Scepticism, non-conformity and independence in thinking:** The creative person is never satisfied with the things as they are, but always tries to improve upon them. Being original, divergent and independent in his thinking, he becomes sceptical of the old ideas and welcomes the new ones. He becomes a non-conformist and unconventional in his approach.

- **Persistence:** The creative person has the tendency to be fully absorbed in his work. He accepts challenges and shows interest in solving difficult tasks and problems. He is found to work hard, long time even at odd hours.
- **Risk-taking:** The creative child has the tendency to take calculated risks because of being self-confident and independent thinking. He enjoys the meeting of challenge and expressing new ideas. He can take chances to experiment and is not afraid of failures.
- **Humour:** A high sense of humour is another important indicator of creative potential. In a comparative study of high creative and high I. Q. groups, the highly creative students were found to be significantly more humorous than the high I. Q. students.

Creativity is not a unitary trait but a complex of so many discrete abilities and personality qualities. Potentials for creative production in different field are not same in quality and quantity. Creativity to the artist is the ability to evoke an emotional mood.

To the architect, creativity is the ability to evolve new approaches, forms and new materials. To the scientist, creativity is the ability to explore new way of extending knowledge and so on.

1.4 Development of Creativity

There are two different views regarding the development of creativity. One view is that all mental abilities are hereditary and cannot be developed (Galton, 1869), while the other view describes that mental abilities are kinds of skills which can be developed through appropriate education and training (Guilford, 1962; Parnes and Brunelle, 1967; Torrance, 1972; Rose and Lin, 1984).

Torrance (1967) is of the opinion that heredity does not place limits upon creative development and achievement. Like sense organs, peripheral nervous system and brain, creative abilities are also inherited. How these abilities develop and function, however, is strongly influenced by the way the environment responds to a person's curiosity and creativity needs. It indicates that the environmental influences are more important in the development of creativity. Even if we assume that creative thinking abilities are hereditary, the expression of creative potential will depend upon the environmental influences. It means that the degree of creative expression can be increased by the environmental manipulation [Gupta, 2006].

Torrance (1962), reviewing a number of studies on the growth of creativity and findings of many studies conducted by himself at Minnesota, has described the length of development of creative abilities. The following are some general conclusions drawn on the basis of these studies:

- **Ages Two to Four:** During the two-to-four years old period, the child learns about the world through direct experience, and repetition of his experiences in verbal and imaginative play. He thrills over the wonders of nature. His curiosity about his environment continues, and he explores it in his own unique way. The child needs the freedom to explore, helps of parents to remove obstacles and opportunities for doing things.
- **Ages Four to Six:** Ligon (1957) and his associates say that the typical child from four to six has a good imagination but they do not make any observations about a lessening of imagination which other have found at about the middle of this period. At this age, he starts to become aware of the feelings of and begins thinking how his actions will affect others. The kindergarten period is very much crucial.
- **Ages Six to Eight:** According to him, the creative imagination of the child between six and eight takes a turn towards realism to the extent that he tries to reproduce details even in play. His curiosity continues to develop and his school experiences are challenging and rewarding. Children enjoy creating characters and making others guess who they are. They should be encouraged

to go as far as they can on a project work with their new ideas.

- **Ages Eight to Ten:** The child between eight to ten is increasingly able to use a variety of skills in being creative and can discover ways for using his unique abilities creatively. He likes to identify with heroes to use his imagination and other skills to help his friends. He needs opportunities to express his originality and ingenuity.
- **Ages Ten to Twelve**: Artistic and musical aptitudes are developing rapidly at this age. The child of this ages should be given opportunities to explore, to build, to make, to read and to communicate to others about his experiences. The child needs to test out his ideas and skills.
- **Ages Twelve to Fourteen:** The twelve-to-fourteen years old youth tends to be concerned with the activities of the moment and rarely plans for the future. During this stage, gifted children produce remarkable performances in imaginative, artistic, musical, and mechanical fields. The youth feels insecure, however, because of changes in his physical and emotional make-up and a growing strangeness in interpersonal relations. It is a time to give him experience in making decisions and carrying them out.
- **Ages Fourteen to Sixteen:** Between the ages of fourteen and sixteen much of the imaginative activity seems to be focused on a future career. Adventure is still the keyword for all phases of life for both sexes. Sometimes youth realise that there are no appropriate solutions to some problems but he is not capable to apply the principles creatively which he has learned.
- **Ages Sixteen to Eighteen:** The youth of this stage, needs to give his imagination full rein, as he sorts what is and is not important, according to Ligon (1957). He can learn to channel emotional energy creatively, solve problems and

participate more vigorously in groups. Various tests of interest, abilities and attitudes toward life can be useful. The concept that emotional energy can be used creatively or destructively should be introduced and tested. After High School creative development is not so remarkable [Torrance, 1969].

Necessity of Early Detection of Creativity:

Researchers have shown that unless detected and nurtured at an early age, many of the capabilities and talents either go waste for ever or, if the attempt is made to cultivate them later on, they cannot be developed fully. It is very essential, therefore, that a search for creative potential in children is made from the earliest possible stage.

Perhaps the most convincing argument in this context seems to emerge from an analysis of the developmental trend of creative potential. Although the results of various studies including Indian studies concerning developmental stages of creativity have varied in results, a general trend is to be noted. Whenever creativity is not identified at the early stage and opportunities for creative expression and development were lacking, there was a drop in the developmental curve. This phenomenon of slump in creative thinking has been attributed to lack of proper identification and opportunities.

1.5 Environment and Creativity

Development of creativity needs favourable environment. If the child is provided with conducive environment to the development of creative potential, his creativity can develop to the maximum. A positive environment or situation that is open, democratic and free may be said to contribute positively to the release and development of creative potential. On the other hand, a closed society, culture or situation may act as a strong deterrent to the development of initiative within the individual. Arieti (1976) proposed the concept of creativogenic society to emphasize the influence of culture and environment on the development of creativity. According to him, the creativogenic society or environment is distinguished by its lack of emphasis on immediate gratification, its tolerance for and interest in divergent points of view, and its use of incentives and rewards for creativity.

There is a need for properly planned, deliberate and conscious efforts on the part of teachers, parents, members of the family, Government as well as the children themselves for the appropriate nurturing and stimulation of the creative urge and potential. Therefore, it should be ensured that children are provided with the environment and facilities conducive to the nurturing and stimulation of all that which is helpful in the development of creativity, and qualities like originality, flexibility, fluency, divergent thinking and sensitivity [Mangal, 2005].

Development of creativity depends upon many environmental factors particularly related to home, school and society. Home is a social unit that exerts the greatest influence on the development of the child's behaviour. At home, parents are usually the most important persons in building the psycho-social climate of the entire family. Parents' interaction pattern, attitudes, values create the home environment for a child.

1.6 Family Environment and Creativity

Many research studies on creativity show that families play a very important role in the realization of promise and potential (Bloom, 1985). Ellermeyer (1993) reminds us that, "parents can directly influence the development of creativity in their children by promoting fantasy in play and curiosity in the early childhood years. Parents of creative pre-schoolers are generally conceptually abstract thinkers, patient, flexible, open-minded, insightful and afford their children a high degree of independence". The following environments or factors are conducive to the development and nurturance of creativity of the children:

- Non-authoritarian attitudes of parents are needed to develop their children's creativity. When parents open-minded, welcome different opinion on a particular problem, when they neither insist on conformity nor criticise children for expressing new ideas or doing new things and discuss creative efforts with children, creativity flourishes.

- Emotional support at home, especially during early ages, can facilitate the expression and development of creativity. Parents will reduce the fearfulness and anxiety on their part to help them in creative thinking.
- Parents should give their children the freedom to explore, think, act, experiment and express their views and feelings independently.
- Parents may try to help their children to engage in creative activities, provide support to different new and unusual ideas.
- Discipline should not be very strict to aid creative expression but it must be consistent.
- Parents first need to find out the field in which their child shows a fairly good amount of creativity and they can provide a variety of creative experiences related to the concerned area.
- Parents need to express their happiness when unusual curious questions come from their child who demands answers, explanation as well as elaboration. To strengthen creative thinking of their child, parents may appreciate or give material rewards also.
- Parents should give a variety of sources and situations to their child in the field of his interest and hobbies.
- Some research findings show significant positive relationships between creativity and role-models. The child may accept and internalise the qualities of his role models.

Deshmukh (1977) has listed four type of activities, namely; ***searching, organizing, originating,*** and ***communication*** for creating a conducive environment for the development of creativity. Torrance (1961) has emphasized reward as a crucial factor in maintaining creative atmosphere. He has given five principles for rewarding creative thinking:

1) Treat unusual questions with respect,
2) Treat unusual ideas with respect,
3) Show children that their ideas have values,
4) Provide opportunities for self-initiated learning and give credit for it.
5) Provide periods of non-evaluated practice.

On the other hand, some factors are against the creativity nurturing or development. These are anti-creativity factors which are as follows:

- Harsh and forced discipline.
- Indifference to creative efforts.
- Forcing students to believe in what the teacher / parents say.
- Giving so much home work that students are unable to think over problems.
- No scope for independent study.
- Discouraging students when they think divergently.
- Providing negative reinforcement when students express opinions against teacher's views.
- Discouraging questions from students.
- Assuming all students to be alike.
- Group pressures to conformity.
- Encouraging intelligent students only.
- Monotonous classroom activities and assignment.

- Over dependence on guidebooks and evaluation system in formal education.

One or more of these anti-creativity factors may blocked the divergent thinking processes. Therefore, these should be removed as far as possible.

Family environment consists of its several components, such as, family structure, socio-economic status, family tension, interpersonal relationship among the members, stress and anxiety of the members etc. Most of them are created by and depended on the activities of the parents or major family members. Therefore, psycho-emotional climate of the families is very different for different families. This situation or condition affects the abilities of the child, especially, in the development or nurturing the creativity.

1.6.1 Socio-economic Status and Creativity

A child is born and brought up in the socio-emotional climate of the family. With the natural growth and development of the child, the innate creative potential obtained by heredity is gradually being unfolded or developed if the emotional climate is favourable to it. The Socio-economic Status (which covers mainly, Education, Occupation and Income) may influence the favourable environment for unfolding creative potential. Studies made by Pandey, R. C. (1981), Singh, R. P. (1980) and John, C. D. (1988) show that Creativity and its components are related with Socio-economic Status. Again, Halpin, Payne and Ellett (1973) found that Socio-economic Status positively related to the creativity of boys not girls.

Runco, M. A. (2004) has described the influence of Socio-economic Status (SES) on creativity. He said that unlike academic success, creativity seems to flourish in larger families. The reason for this may be that children in larger families spend more time without supervision and thus need to use their own imaginative skills to remain entertained or it is a result of frequent and playful child-child interaction in larger family.

Creative thinking is related to socio-economic status, for larger families tend to come from lower socio-economic levels, they may then have fewer toys and environmental distractions. They then could be creative in finding ways to play which increases their original thinking. Again, more siblings in the family teach them to share, divide and play in variety of ways. So, it helps to develop flexibility in their thinking.

Dudek *et al.* (1993) shows that socio-economic status (SES) contributed to creative thinking during an individual's developmental years, with higher socio-economic status being beneficial to creativity. Though "necessity is the mother of invention", the alternative - that some necessities are common in lower SES levels and stimulate creative thinking - has not been supported empirically, at least not directly.

Families communicate cultural values to their children, and are responsible for their socialization and culturalization. In a sense, family's channel and select culture for their children [Albert, 1991].

Socio-economic status is relevant to creativity and its development in parts because socio-economic status determines what kinds of experiences and resources will be available in the family. Additionally, parental education is correlated with family socio-economic status. Parental education by itself plays a large role in development of creativity. Socio-economic status may also determine how wide range of experiences a child will have in travelling or in reading books.

1.6.2 Freedom of Thought and Actions and Creativity

Freedom of thought and actions enjoyed by the child in the family may be considered as an aspect of family environment. Parents should help the child to find his own identity and allow him for open expression of ideas and independent thought; reduce parent-child identification, but not necessarily affiliation or affection, provide support in the presence of challenges, which aids in the development of creativity and good mental health. Parents need to establish and maintain bonds with children, also allow them autonomy, independence and psychological and emotional space.

Research findings suggest that a good family environment is responsible to develop a unique individual who could express his/her thoughts and feelings freely. Individuals who come from such families are more likely to be very creative, as well as highly competent, in their work. Such families foster creativity and intellectual risk taking. The circumstances within homes and families that create environments conducive to the development of independent identities and thought are many and varied. In such environment parents include anything to reduce parent-child identification and build an "emotional space" between child and parent, children are less monitored and directed by their parents. These conditions make the children more independent, autonomous, and less sex-stereotyped [Olszewski-Kubilius, 2001].

1.6.3 Gender Difference and Creativity

In Indian Family culture, unfortunately, yet, boys and girls are not treated in the same way in various aspects. Hence, children's creativity development may be varied with their gender difference. A few studies have concerned themselves with gender differences in creativity, the results were not equivocal. Prakash (1966), Raina (1969) reported that boys were more creative than girls. However, Pareek (1966), Hussain (1974), Hargreaves (1977) found no difference between the creativity of boys and girls. Singh (1978), on the other hand, found that girls were better than boys on tests will semantic content.

Raina (1971) and Goyal (1974) found that females were significantly superior to males only on fluency and flexibility dimensions of creativity. Again, Singh (1978), reported that female students were superior to male students in fluency and originality dimensions of creativity.

Male students were found to be significantly superior to their female counterparts on verbal creativity (Prakash, 1966, Gagneja,1972, Jain,1971, Sharma, 1979). On the non-verbal creativity, too, the male students were significantly superior to female students. Passi (1972) with respect to different dimensions of creativity, reported that male students were significantly higher than female students in Originality.

Sex differences are not always found in assessment of creativity, though historical analyses do uncover differences that may reflect bias and favoritism. Reis described how the developmental and career paths of women are more diverse than those of men. She also concluded that relationships play a larger role in women's creative efforts than in men's creative efforts.

Sarkar (1994) has found that sex was a contributing factor to creativity and its different components. Boys and girls mostly differ from one another on the scores of creativity. He also found that boys are superior to girls in creativity scores. Thus, overall reviews regarding gender difference in creativity do not make any conclusion.

1.7 The Present Problem

Many research findings have consistently shown that all children have the potential to think creatively and the development of creativity has been influenced by the factors of environment. Among the three types of environments (*Family, School and Social environments*), family environment has much influences on the development of creativity in the children. In most of the research works to establish the relationship with creativity, creativity of the children has been assessed either verbal form or non-verbal form of tests. Again, if the creative productions are the results of family environment-factors, how much do they contribute to it? Furthermore, in this society how are the factors of family environment correlated with creativity? The answers were not clear to the present researcher.

The present researcher considered Socio-economic Status and Freedom of thought and actions – as the aspects of family environment to find out the relationships with creativity. Also, the creativity of the children had been assessed by using both verbal tests and non-verbal tests of creativity.

Again, between boys and girls, who would be more creative in this context?

In this society, which aspect of family environment would be the greatest contributor to fluency, flexibility and originality component of creativity. Hence, considering the above issues, the title of the present research was as follows:

> ***"Creativity in Relation to Freedom and Socio-economic Status in Family Environment".***

1.8 Statement of the Problem

The main purpose of this study was to find out the relationship between components of creativity and aspects of family environment (Socio-economic Status, and Freedom of thought and actions) of school going students in the Districts of Nadia and 24 Parganas (North)- where various kind of people live. Thus, the problem was stated as:

> ***"Creativity in Relation to Freedom and Socio-economic Status in Family Environment".***

1.9 Rationale of the Problem

Creativity is one of the most highly valued qualities of human beings, because its contribution to society is enormous.

So long, studies on creativity have been done with the primary focus on the intellectual aspect of personality or any other trait of personality. A few research works have been conducted on creativity in experimental aspect, that is, training creativity or development of creativity. But how the family environment influences creativity in children and what relationship exists between creativity and various aspects of family environment were not properly explored. This type of research was important in the sense that it might help to create suitable family environment for nurturing creativity in children.

Economic condition is an important determinant of family environment. At the same time, social status of an individual leads him to react in a particular way. So, Socio-economic Status of a family reflects the whole environment of the family proportionately. Hence the researcher considered Socio-economic Status as the variable for this study.

Freedom of thought and actions enjoyed by the children in the family may be related with the components of creativity. Freedom to play, freedom to make various things, models may increase their flexibility and originality components of creativity.

In these regards, the present researcher considered Socio-economic Status and Freedom of thought and actions as the independent variables for this study.

According to Piaget (1952), the formal operational stage of intellectual development in children comes at the age of 11 and above. This is the stage when the child can think in abstract terms, follow logical propositions and reasons for hypothesis. He can separate the components of a problem and can logically explore all possible solutions to problems. So, the researcher considered Class VIII and Class IX students as samples for this study.

Each of the two districts – Nadia and 24 Parganas (North) of West Bengal has a diversified area which includes a part of A-1 city, sub-urban areas, municipalities, many villages, industrial areas, business markets, rivers and fertile cultivated lands. Various types of professions are found among the people of each district. Environment of these families, no doubt, are very different in all respects. So, when the students of these families would be treated as sample it must be of different types. Hence, the researcher considered all the students of Class VIII and IX of Bengali medium schools of two districts as the population of the study.

1.10 Objectives of the Study

The objectives of the present study were framed as follows:

1) To assess the verbal and non-verbal creativity of all the students in terms of fluency, flexibility and originality.

2) To study the gender difference in different components - fluency, flexibility and originality of both verbal and non-verbal creativity.

3) To study the difference between Freedom and Restriction group boys in fluency, flexibility and originality of both verbal and non-verbal creativity.

4) To study the difference between Freedom and Restriction group girls in fluency, flexibility and originality of both verbal and non-verbal creativity.

5) To study the difference between High and Low Socio-economic Status group boys in different components - fluency, flexibility and originality of both verbal and non-verbal creativity.

6) To study the difference between High and Low Socio-economic Status group girls in different components - fluency, flexibility and originality of both verbal and non-verbal creativity.

7) To study the relationship between Freedom of students and different components of both verbal and non-verbal creativity for boys.

8) To study the relationship between Freedom of students and different components of both verbal and non-verbal creativity for girls.

9) To study the relationship between Socio-economic Status and different components of both verbal and non-verbal creativity for boys.

10) To study the relationship between Socio-economic Status and different components of both verbal and non-verbal creativity for girls.

11) To develop a Multiple Regression Equation of Total Fluency on Freedom of students, Socio-economic Status.

12) To develop a Multiple Regression Equation of Total Flexibility on Freedom of students, Socio-economic Status.

13) To develop a Multiple Regression Equation of Total Originality on Freedom of students, Socio-economic Status.

14) To explain an ideal family environment for better development of creativity in children.

1.11 Significance of the Study

Creativity is one of the most important qualities of human beings, because it alone can enhance development in all directions and lead to social progress. The countries where the development of creativity in individuals has been encouraged are now in better positions in respect of economic prosperity and national development.

Traditional education system always emphasizes on the ability of convergent thinking rather than the ability of divergent thinking. So, most of the parents, the teachers and the other family members always try to encourage and reward for better development in convergent thinking such as memorizing the facts and obtaining better marks in the examination and not for divergent thinking. But now it is very important to make understand the people about the necessity of development of divergent thinking as well as creative thinking. At the same time, they should know what kind of family environment is favourable for fostering creative potential in their children in this social perspective. Again, which factors of the family make an ideal environment for promoting creativity in the children, should be determined. Therefore, establishing the relationship between aspects of family environment and components of creativity are very important. From these points of view, the study has got immense significance.

1.12 Operational Definitions of the Terms Used

The operational definitions of the terms used in this study were given below for proper understanding:

i) **Creativity:** In this study, creativity operationally defined as the ability to bring something new into given situations or problems. It includes person's behavioural characteristics like fluency, flexibility and originality.

ii) **Fluency:** Fluency is the ability of an individual to produce a large number of ideas within a particular time period. When the responses are in words, it is called verbal fluency and when the responses are in figural form, it is called non-verbal fluency.

iii) **Flexibility:** It is the ability of an individual to produce a variety of different ideas within specific time period. In case of word responses, it is called verbal flexibility and in case of figural form, it is called non-verbal flexibility.

iv) **Originality:** It is the ability of an individual to produce unusual ideas or rarer responses. Verbal originality score is obtained from the word responses and non-verbal originality score is obtained from the figural responses.

v) **Aspects of Family Environment:** In this study, aspects of family environment are defined as the determinants or factors which influence the family environment. It also includes the scope created in the family environment. In this study, it includes Socio-economic Status of the family, and Freedom of thought and actions enjoyed by the student in the family only.

vi) **Socio-economic Status:** It is the status of the family regarding economic condition and social status. In this study, it is scored on the basis of occupation of parents, monthly income, educational qualification, condition of the home and materials possession.

vii) **Freedom:** Freedom means freedom of thought and actions enjoyed by the child in the family.

1.13 Hypotheses of the Study

In both verbal and non-verbal test the criterion of creativity is an independent measurement of Fluency, originality and Flexibility.

Keeping in mind the objectives of the present study and findings of the review of related studies, the researcher formulated the following hypotheses:

H_1: There would be no significant difference between boys and girls in Fluency scores of verbal and non-verbal creativity.

H_2: There would be no significant difference between boys and girls in Flexibility scores of verbal and non-verbal creativity.

H_3: There would be no significant difference between boys and girls in Originality scores of verbal and non-verbal creativity.

H_4: There would be significant difference between Freedom and Restriction group boys in Fluency, Flexibility and Originality scores of verbal and non-verbal creativity.

H_5: There would be significant difference between Freedom and Restriction group girls in Fluency, Flexibility and Originality scores of verbal creativity.

H_6: There would be significant difference between Freedom and Restriction group girls in Fluency, Flexibility and Originality scores of non-verbal creativity.

H_7: There would be significant difference between High and Low Socio-economic Status group boys in Fluency, Flexibility and Originality scores of verbal and non-verbal creativity.

H_8: There would be significant difference between High and Low Socio-economic Status group girls in Fluency, Flexibility and Originality scores of verbal and non-verbal creativity.

H_9: There would be significant relationship between Freedom of students and components of creativity (Fluency, Flexibility, Originality) of both verbal and non-verbal creativity tests for boys.

H_{10}: There would be significant relationship between Freedom of students and components of verbal creativity (Fluency, Flexibility, Originality) for girls.

H_{11}: There would be significant relationship between Freedom of students and components of non-verbal creativity (Fluency, Flexibility, Originality) of both verbal and non-verbal creativity tests for girls.

H_{12}: There would be significant relationship between Socio-economic Status and components of verbal creativity (Fluency, Flexibility, Originality) for boys.

H_{13}: There would be significant relationship between Socio-economic Status and components of non-verbal creativity (Fluency, Flexibility, Originality) for boys.

H_{14}: There would be significant relationship between Socio-economic Status and components of creativity (Fluency, Flexibility, Originality) of both verbal and non-verbal creativity tests for girls.

H_{15}: Freedom of students, Socio-economic Status would be significant predictors of Total Fluency.

H_{1}: Freedom of students, Socio-economic Status would be significant predictors of Total Flexibility.

H_{17} Freedom of students, Socio-economic Status would be significant predictors of Total Originality.

1.14 Delimitations of the Study

In order to conduct the study, the researcher delimited the planning of his investigation which were stated below:

Population

All the students of class VIII and IX of Bengali medium schools under West Bengal Board of Secondary Education of districts Nadia and North 24 Parganas, West Bengal, were the population for the present study. Only Government aided schools were considered in this study. Thus, English or Hindi medium schools under West Bengal Board of Secondary Education or any other Board, private schools were not included in this population.

Sample

The study is limited to the sample of 372 school going students of class VIII and class IX selected from eight different types of schools of district Nadia and North 24 Parganas.

Schools

Total eight Bengali medium schools were selected out of which one Boys' school, one Girls' school and two Co-education types schools from each of the two districts were considered only.

Aspects of Family Environment

In this study, only four aspects of family environment were considered. They were as follows:

i) Socio-economic Status

ii) Freedom of thought and actions.

Components of Creativity

Only three components of creativity had been considered in this study, such as –

i) Fluency

ii) Flexibility

iii) Originality

Form of Creativity Test

Considering time duration of the tests administration in the classroom, intermediate form of Sarker's Creativity Test had been used for assessment of creativity of the students in this study.

Gender

Stratification with respect to gender is necessary for comparative study. For this reason, the researcher included both boys and girls in the sample of the study.

2

REVIEW OF RELATED LITERATURE

Review of the related literature allows the researcher to acquaint himself with current knowledge in that field. A careful review of the research journals, books, dissertations, thesis and other resources of information on the problem to be investigated is one of the important steps in planning any research study. It serves the following specific objectives:

1. To enable the researcher to define the limits of the study.

Review of related literature helps the researcher to delimit and define the problem. The knowledge of related literature enables the researcher to state the objectives of the study very clearly and concisely.

2. To avoid useless problem areas.

The researcher can select those areas for the research study which are useful and significant for the society.

3. To avoid unintentional duplication of well-established findings.

Review of related literature helps the researcher to acquire knowledge of the findings in that area so that the researcher can avoid the duplication of any study.

4. To get the appropriate methodology.

After reviewing the related literature, the researcher is enabled to select the useful and appropriate research methodology for the study.

5. To know previous recommendations.

The important reason for review of related literature is to know about the recommendations for further research given by the earlier researchers in that particular field.

2.1 Researches on Creativity in General

The review of creativity implies that it is reactive; and surely, it often is a reaction to problems or challenges. Yet creativity is also one of the prime factors of cultural evolution. Runco (2004) of Psychology Department, California State University, California, has reviewed some researches on creativity in the Annual Review of Psychology, with various dimensions. Runco mentioned the following in the review studies:

Bruner (1962) claimed that we must encourage the creativity of our children and students as preparation for the future, given that the future is more difficult than ever before to define. Given the "greying of America", it will come as no surprise that more and more research is exploring life span creativity. The research reviewed suggests that creativity facilitates late-life adaptations and growth (Cohen 1989; Dudek & Hall 1991; Runco & Charles 1997). This is especially true of the flexibility allowed by creativity, because older adults tend to rely on routines and, unless intentionally creative, become inflexible (Rubenson & Runco 1995).

Although a number of excellent studies of creative talents and creative persons were published before 1950, a great deal of credit is given to J. P. Guilford (1950). His presidential address to the American Psychological Association was titled "Creativity", and his argument at that time, and his subsequent empirical efforts, went a long way toward convincing individual of the possibility of being scientific about the creativity. Guildford also argued convincingly that creativity was a vital "natural resource".

Barron & Harrington (1981) devoted most of their review to (a) creativity in relation to intelligence, and (b) creativity and personality. The relationship between creativity and intelligence has been researched since 1981. Personality is also being studied, but many other influences on creative work have been identified. Some of these are tied to the individual's potentials, dispositions, abilities and capacities and some are tied to the environment and social context. Runco reviewed the researches on creativity reflecting different disciplinary assumptions. He reviewed the behavioural perspective on creativity, researches on the biology of creativity, clinical, cognitive, developmental, economic, educational, historiometric, organizational, psychometric and social researches. These approaches overlap a great deal, and an interdisciplinary perspective is the best. Because several important topics do not fit neatly into either the alternative or the disciplinary categorization.

Amabile & Gryskiewiez (1989) and later Witt & Beorkrem (1989) identified the following "situational influences on creativity: freedom, autonomy, good role models and resources, encouragement specially for originality, freedom from criticism, and "norms in which innovation is prized and failure not fatal" (Will & Beorkrem, pp. 31 – 32). Some influences can also inhibit creativity. These include a lack of respect (specially for originality), red tape, constraint, lack of autonomy and resources, inappropriate norms, project management, feedback, time pressure, competition, and unrealistic expectations. Murray (1998) identified the alpha and beta presses, one being objective and one being subjective. Competition is a good example of how these may differ, for competition may both stimulate and inhibit creative work (Watson, 1968); its impact depends on the individual's interpretation. The same may hold true for resources, at least in the sense that creative insights may sometimes absolutely require resources, but sometimes result from paucity.

Time is indeed an important resource. Mednick (1962), for example, suggested that original ideas are remote and well removed from the original problem or initial idea. This remoteness requires time; it takes time to move from idea to idea and to find the "remote associate". A number of empirical studies have confirmed Mednick's (1962) predictions. Time is also important for incubation, though here it is time away from a task rather than devoted to it.

The role of press in the creative process also can be seen in the research on family background. Most work in this area seems to focus on family structure, in contrast to family process. The relevant structural variables include birth order, family size and number of siblings, and age gap. Sulloway (1996) for instance, presented data showing that middle children are the most rebellious, and are therefore potentially creative (Gaynor & Runco, 1992). Albert & Runco (1989) reported that the autonomy within a family, not just the number of siblings or family structure, could dramatically influence creativity. Very likely, family structure has an impact on development of creativity because it determines family processes. Larger families have more authoritarian parents, just to name one example of how structure can determine process.

Some recent research suggests that environmental designs for schools are conducive to creativity (Hasirci & Demirkan, 2003). Although it would be best to design an environment on an individual-by-individual basis, all other things being equal, environments should allow independent work, be stimulating but not distracting and easy access to resources. These findings align well with those in the organizational setting (Amabile, 2003; Witt & Beorkrem, 1989).

The product approach to creativity focuses on outcomes and those things that result from the creative process. The assumption here is that studies of products (e.g., publications, paintings, poems, designs) are highly objective, and therefore amenable to the scientific method. Products can be counted, for example, and sometimes it is just the quantity of one's efforts that is measured. The value of this approach is supported by the amazing productivity of Piaget, Picasso and other luminaries (Simonto, 1984). The problem with this approach is that it often informs us only about productivity and not about creativity. Also, it can be quite misleading because what it takes to be productive may differ from what it takes to be creative. An individual can be productive without being original and originality is the most widely acknowledged requisite for creativity. In methodological terms, productivity and creativity are correlated but not synonymous [Runco, 2004, pp. 661 - 663].

Sex differences can be explained in terms of family background, though biology is a strong influence as well. Sex differences are not always found in assessments of creativity, though historical analyses do uncover differences that may reflect bias and favoritism. There does seem to be a benefit in being raised in a psychologically androgynous fashion (Harrington *et al.*, 1983) rather than as a stereotypical male or female. The androgynous individual may have more options available when solving problems, rather than just options that are stereotypically masculine or feminine, and he or she may be more flexible than the stereotyped male or female.

Early family experiences may help explain differences between boys and girls (Baer, 2003; Tegano & Moran, 1989), but it is also now clear that sex differences also reflect life span discrepancies between man and woman (Helson, 1990; Reis, 1999). Reis described how the developmental and career paths of women are more diverse than those of men. She also concluded that the relationships play a larger role in women's creative efforts than in men's creative efforts [Runco, 2004; p. 669].

Dudek *et al.* (1993) felt that socioeconomic status (SES) contributed to creative thinking during an individual's developmental years, with higher SES being beneficial to creativity. Though "necessity is the mother of invention", the alternative - that some necessities are common in lower SES levels and stimulate creative thinking - has not been supported empirically, at least not directly.

According to Runco (2004), the categories of research (i.e., person, process, and press and the disciplinary categories) suggest that in many ways creativity research has broadened its scope in the past 20 years. It is now more of an interdisciplinary effort than even before, and new techniques, topics and applications are apparent in the research. The field is also more focused and more selective. It is not easy to pinpoint exactly how it is selective. The selection that has occurred within the field may be best viewed as topical, and perhaps due to the current zeitgeist.

Feist & Runco (1993) examined researches published in the *Journal of Creative Behaviour* between 1969 and 1989. They found a decrease in the attention being given to personality and an increase in social research and educational studies of creativity. They also examined *Psychological Abstracts* for the 1980s and discovered that approximately 0.01% of the abstracts involved creativity and they also found that approximately 9000 works on creativity were published between 1960 and 1991.

Faizi et al. (2013) drew some principles on findings of their work titled *"Design Guidelines of Residential Environments to Stimulate Children's Creativity"* published in Journal of Asian Behavioural Studies. The effective variables of their study were—

1. Stimulation of the natural environmental elements: The research showed that using of natural elements (water, light, and plants), the child's curiosity and excitement for the play can be increased.
2. Child's Play and Participation: This factor is associated by participation rate of children for any change in the space, for example, their participation in planting and maintaining flowering areas, drawing on the walls and their participation in changing the decoration.
3. Flexibility of functions: The purpose of flexibility is to provide one or more solution adapted to the context of the application in order to provide the ideal solution. By changing special aspect of housing, a space can proportionately be used.
4. Curiosity: The purpose of curiosity is to encourage children to ask questions and learn. The children try to find the answers. The principles drawn from the findings of their study were:

Principle 1: "connectedness and continuity of open and closed spaces (natural spaces)".

Principle 2: "a free plan design form and presence of small walls or movable partition walls that children create places for themselves by help of their parents".

Principle 3: "to create diversity by natural elements". Natural landscape has a correlation with creativity potential. Creativity level can be increased through the existence of plant in the interiors.

Principle 4: "play making by natural elements".

Using the aforementioned principles in designing the residential spaces can be prepared the base of increasing the curiosity and "play-participation", and thus improving the child's creativity by applying the variables such as "natural stimulus elements" and "flexibility of functions".

Edwards (2012) mentioned some aspects of home environment in the study titled "A Family's Role in Developing Creativity at Home". Those were as follows:

- provide many possibilities for cooperative role-play that children can change at their whim.
- encourage children to create games with spontaneity, without family interference.
- always have materials and items available for children to engage in "secretive" play, such as a blanket thrown over an old card table.
- provide toys that promote creativity by allowing children to explore and discover, such as hard wooden blocks.

Olszewski-Kubilius (2001) explores parenting strategies in *"The social and emotional development of gifted children: What do we know?"* that seem to work best with gifted young people. It acknowledges that no child or family is the same but draws conclusions from commonalities that exist in the families of profoundly gifted young people who have been able to pursue their talents. It offers suggestions to parents such as letting the child experience some stresses in life and also letting them make their own decisions.

Parents enact their values (Olszewski et al., 1987). They can demonstrate a love of work and learning. They make independent learning outside of structured or traditional activities and settings. Parents also help to make children's personality dispositions which are necessary elements to talent development such as their coping up abilities with the failure as well as risk taking. They advise children that in order to gain success there need so much hard work and have to consistent with it longer period of time.

Another very important role for parents is helping their talented children build social networks that can give them emotional support for their abilities and talent development activities (Subotnik & Olszewski-Kubilius, 1997). Social networks consist of the people within a child's life and their interconnections. Social interconnectedness affects the psychological and physical elements of the individuals and the size and members of the society also affect for the same. The social world of the child begins with the family; but, over time, as higher levels of talent development are achieved, it expands to include teachers, coaches, mentors, and a wider scope of peers. Participation in special activities, such as competitions or after-school and summer programs, can augment and populate social networks with peers who provide specific emotional support for achievement in the talent domain. Friends and companions who are also involved in the talent field can be essential to sustaining commitment during critical times [Subotnik & Olszewski-Kubilius].

While research generally supports the positive role families can play in developing talent, the literature also suggests that different kinds of family dynamics yield different outcomes for children. Specifically, family dynamics greatly influence children's motivations to achieve or produce, and different patterns of family attitudes, behaviors, and parenting styles may create different kinds of motivations. Creatively gifted children are found to have families that stress independence, rather than interdependence, between family members; are less child-centered; have somewhat tense family relationships (ones with "wobble"); and have more expressions of negative affect and competition between family members, resulting in motivation toward power and dominance (Albert, 1978, 1983). Strong family cohesiveness and child-centered environment within the family gives birth to the high scholastic achievers and high levels of motivation for the achievement.

Studies suggest that an important family-environment factor is the degree to which the family creates an atmosphere where children are free to develop a unique identity and have their own individual thoughts and express them freely. Children who come from such family environments are naturally very creative and competent in their work. Such families foster creativity and intellectual risk taking. The circumstances within homes and families that create environments conducive to the development of independent identities and thought are many and varied. They include anything that results in a reduction in parent-child identification, an "emotional space" between parent and child, lower levels of parental monitoring of children, and less conventional socialization of children by parents. From the research findings it is suggested that "Space" include both positive and negative influence on the children, sometimes it develops imbalance in parental and family relationship and sometimes they being less involved with children create favourable environment for children to grow (Ochse, 1993; Olszewski-Kubilius, 1997). These conditions are thought to result in children being more independent, autonomous, and less sex-stereotyped. They also cause children to retreat from interpersonal relationships at home (if very difficult circumstances exist) or contribute to the development of a preference for time alone (if more benign circumstances exist), resulting in more time and opportunity for both practice and skill acquisition in the talent area and a rich internal fantasy life (Ochse, 1993; Simonton, 1992).

Although research on eminent individuals seems to suggest that family stress and unhappy childhoods can be major components of the process of producing a creative individual, are they necessary ingredients? Not according to C sikszentmihalyi, Rathunde, and Whalen, (1993), who talked about a balance of support and tension is needed within the family which is conducive to the development of high levels of talent and good mental health. They made the point that, because researchers studying families of talented individuals have lacked a conceptual classification for families with a balance of support and tension, they did not study or looked for these kinds of families. These families provide contexts for children that are both integrated (family members are connected and supportive of one another), yet also differentiated (there were high expectations from parents that each child would develop his/her talent to the highest possible degree and would express his/her encouragement of individual thought and expression). Such families produce autotelic personalities in children or individuals who are self-motivated and self-directed. According to Csikszentmihalyi, Rathunde, and Whalen, an overemphasis on one of the characteristics of these can develop in individuals who are either very much creative or talented, but not very well-adjusted (primacy of differentiation), or very well adjusted, but not creative or talented (primacy of integration). It may be that high levels of talent development needs motivation which had developed through childhood tragedy perhaps arose from good psychological development; other levels of both talent and mental health result from a more balanced blend of tension or challenge and support. Similarly, Therival (1999) also gives emphasis that, for the creative productivity, tragedy and stress does not play as essential elements. He suggested a model of creativity which includes the following components- genetic endowment (G), parental or other "confidence building" assistances (A), and misfortunes (M). It is stated by Therival that creativity can evolve in those individuals whose experience of great misfortunes acts as great assistances present. He distinguished between creators who are dedicated (have high levels of genetic endowment, many assistances in youth, and no major misfortunes) and creators who are "challenged" (have high genetic endowment, some assistances, and some misfortunes). Both could produce creative work but those personalities who are "challenged" are more overtly driven in order to receive recognition and prove themselves. Therival also points out that psychologically abusive childhood challenges which bring out anger can produce less creativity in substantive work [Olszewski-Kubilius, pp.205-212].

Norah Al-sulaiman (2009) has done a study on "Cross-Cultural Studies And Creative Thinking Abilities" and he has drawn some valuable conclusions regarding sex difference, family environment and culture. The goal of the study was to provide answers to the following existing research questions by reviewing pertinent studies in the areas of creative development, gender differences, cultural values, family environment, and creativity measurements. These questions were:

1. Are there any differences in the creative development ability of individuals across cultures?
2. Are there differences between males and females in creative thinking across cultural studies?
3. Are there any differences between samples taken from different countries in terms of family environment and creative abilities (i.e., originality, flexibility, fluency, and elaboration, etc.)?
4. What measures of creative thinking differentiate the creative abilities in cross-cultural samples?

Coon (1969) examined gender differences in four cultures: The United States, Germany, Australia, and India. This study analyzed that in the United States, boys could secure higher score on originality in comparison with girls, while girls secure higher score in figural elaboration than the boys. In all other samples, except those collected from India, gender differences were non-significant. In India, boys scored significantly higher than girls in figural originality. This study also involved a comparison of changes in performance between third and fourth grade, on figural, verbal, and total measures. The data showed that the United States sample showed more often a gain from the third grade to the fourth grade, while the reverse was the case for the sample from the other countries in the study, suggesting the importance of cultural factors.

Mar'i (1971) examined that in creative thinking abilities there are the influences of sex differences and cultural differences. The study involved two samples of eighth grade students, one from modern American culture and the other from the Arab rural occupied territories (Palestine). For the assessment of creative thinking Mar'i used Figural B and Verbal B forms of the Torrance Test. His study showed that Arab female students lagged significantly behind boys on all measures of creativity, although male students showed greater variability in performance as compared to females. Within the American sample, no significant sex differences were found, except in fluency and originality on one problem only, and this was in favor of females. In general, the performance of American students was superior to students in the occupied Arab territories and the former showed greater individual differences than the latter. Mar'i explained that individuality is required and encouraged in a modern society while in the other side; individuality is punished in the traditional societies. Further, her study does not mention the stressful conditions that students endure in the occupied territories, which clearly would impact the development of their creative thinking abilities. He also mentioned that the family and the attitude and values of parents have considerable significance in the emergence and development of creative thinking in children, investigators have linked this influence to the degree by which culture encourages or discourages creative thinking. Therefore, creative thinking develop into the children to the extent parents encourage or discourage creative personality characteristics in their children (Busse, 1967; Mackinnon, 1962; Mehrota and Sawers, 1989; Raina, 1980; Strom and Johnson, 1991; and Torrance, 1965).

Mackinnon (1962) indicated that a highly creative person comes from a special kind of home environment, which facilitates the emergence of creative thinking. He reported that he found in studying histories of a sample of highly creative architects that certain aspects of their parents' attitude toward them as children was very important in providing them with opportunities and even necessities in developing qualities of creative performance later in life.

Torrance (1970) studied that six cultures (involving a sample of Black American, White American, Western Australia, Western Samoa, Germany, and India) demonstrated a noticeable reduction in creative thinking abilities of fourth graders. He explained these phenomena by bringing attention to the way children, at about the fourth-grade level, are treated in these cultures and in terms of the kinds of behaviors that are encouraged or discouraged throughout the culture. Furthermore, German, Norwegian, Australian, and Indian groups tended to perform somewhat better on the verbal than on the figural measures, while the Samoan and Black American children functioned at a higher level on the figural measures.

The effect of culture on the creative thinking has been confirmed by Norah-AI-sulaiman from the cross-cultural researches that have been reviewed for this study. Most of the studies indicated that there are significant differences between countries and cultures on creative abilities: originality, fluency, flexibility, and elaboration.

Siddiqi, S. (2011) has published a paper on her research work in *Indian Educational Review* titled "A Comparative Study of Creativity among Boys and Girls of Class VII" where she wished to investigate differences for boys and girls in terms of the relation between different aspects of creativity. Randomly a sample of 50 boys and 50 girls was selected who were studying in two secondary schools of Aligarh city. The investigator had personally met the participants and administered the tool. Torrance Test of Creative thinking (Verbal Form A) designed by E. P. Torrance (1968) was used. Mean S.D.s and T-test were calculated to analyze the data. The findings reveal that in all the variables of verbal creativity boys do not differ significantly from girls, except the measures of originality.

Jinzhen *et al.* (2004) have done a study on Creativity development and family environment. Using creativity test as task and 310 school students aged from 9 to 16 as subjects, this study explored the development of children's creativity and the effect of family environment on creativity. The findings of this study were: (1) Children's creativity increases with their age. But the development of its three dimensions fluency, flexibility and originality - is unbalanced. Compared with other age cohorts, the fluency and flexibility dimensions of creativity develop faster during the age of 9 to 11 years old; (2) Family environment has not only a direct influence but an indirect influence is done via creative attitude.

2.2 Researches on Creativity in India

In India, creativity research is very scanty. It is only in the sixties that researchers in this country began taking any serious interest in this new field.

Creativity research in India had its beginning in 1956 when Bhattacharya conducted a study where he reported that high creatives possessed shallow feeling for life, high sensitivity and ability for logical thinking. Later in 1960, he said that there were two types of creative persons ; of those one are those who are born creatives and the others who have acquired creativity. The Indian research on creativity was further advanced by researchers like Raina (1968), Parmesh (1969), Mehdi (1971), Passi (1971), Goyal (1973), Arora (1974, 1978), Pandey (1980), Sharma (1985), Sarkar (1994) and Gupta (2004).

Manas Roychaudhuri (1963) of the University of Calcutta had done the first research study on creativity for a formal degree. This clinically oriented investigation attempted to lay base the differential psychologic, social-environment and developmental variables that characterised creative talent in music. As Mitra (1975) points out, research in the subject has been receiving serious attention only very recently. Research is relatively new and much remains to be accomplished. According to Raina (1975), what seem to be lacking in much of the work, with some notable exceptions, is preciseness, clarity and maturity of judgement.

In India, it seems that researchers have not been prolific and much has not yet been accomplished in terms of quality and quantity when compared to international contributions. The number of Ph. D. studies rose from 5 (in 1965–1972) to 67 (in 1975–1982). This is indicative the growth of interest in the subject and of the field. However, the number of Ph. D. studies comes down in the years 1983–1987 to 39, which is somewhat surprising. At this stage, it can be asserted that, in India, creativity research has gained popularity and is no longer elementary and fragmentary as was observed in 1971 [Raina, 1975].

Raina (1980) reported several sex differences in creativity over a 10-year period in India. In India in 1959, both figural and verbal tests boys had shown a consistent superiority. Retesting a decade later revealed that the advantage in both verbal and figural creativity had shifted in favour of girls. Raina (1966) conducted a study of creative development in Delhi, India to find out the socio-cultural influences on creative thinking development. He found few differences between boys and girls in the first and second grades, but obtained rather consistent and significant differences between male and female on both the verbal and figural tests from the third grade through the sixth. It is interesting that the results obtained in two different areas (Ajmer and Delhi) are consistent with the results of Torrance's (1966) studies from various parts of the United States, considering that the Indian culture places emphasis on language skills and male superiority. For example, boys in Ajmer and Delhi surpassed girls in the verbal section of creative thinking after grade two. Raina related this result to differential treatment of sexes and the identification of children with sex roles of their culture.

Sarkar, P. (1994) has done a study entitled "A Study of Rural Children : Their Personality Pattern and Creativity". He has found that sex was a contributing factor to creativity and its different components, i.e., boys and girls mostly differ from one another on the scores of creativity and its different components. He also found that boys are superior to girls on the scores of creativity and its components.

Panda (1997) in his study, "Impact of creativity and adjustment on academic achievement", found positive and significant correlations between academic achievement and creativity.

Goel (2004) investigated the effect of home environment on educational aspirations. The sample of the study comprised 100 students (50 boys and 50 girls) of intermediate classes in age groups of 16-20 years. The results revealed that girls had much higher educational aspiration than boys. In comparison to girls, boys felt more rejected with the autocratic atmosphere at home and thinks girls experienced more nurturance than boys.

Pande & Nanda (2005) conducted a study to find the impact of different environment of nursery school on the school readiness of children. In terms of school environment (good/ average/poor) different level or quality of nursery schools were taken and 60 children were taken as sample. Randomly children were taken from 12 nursery schools of Ludhiana district which is situated in Punjab. Results revealed that good school environment improved the level of school readiness of children.

Gupta P. K. (2006) published his valuable research work as a book titled "Education for Creativity: Training, Research and Implication" where he described how the creativity be developed in the VI grade students by giving training. Experimental Design was adopted in the study. Components of both verbal and non-verbal creativity were the dependent variables and Treatment Condition; Intelligence Level and Sex were the independent variables for the study. The Factorial Design was applied for analyzing the data. Major findings of the study were:

- There was no significant interaction of the level of intelligence with Creativity Training Programme on the development of verbal fluency, flexibility and originality.

- Creativity Training Programme is equally effective for both male and female in developing their verbal fluency, flexibility and originality.

Tongper, R. M. (2006) has done a research work on creativity titled "A Study on Creativity among Secondary School Students of Shillong" for Ph. D. degree from North-Eastern Hill University.

Objectives: for the study the major objectives were :

- To determine the divergent production abilities of the secondary school students.
- To study the scientific creativity of the secondary school students.
- To find the differences in the various creativity dimensions by sex, community and types of management.

Sample: 1000 secondary school students studying in class IX were drawn as sample from various secondary schools of Shillong. From all over Shillong, 401 males and 599 females were taken as sample which was drawn from 30 secondary schools.

Methodology: Mean, S. D., Quartile deviation, Skewness and Kurtosis were calculated for the results. At same time 'z' values and Pearson's Product moment Method of correlation were applied in the study.

Major Findings

- No significant difference was observed between male and female secondary school students in their divergent production abilities. But a positive difference was found between the tribal and non-tribal students in that abilities.
- A significant difference was observed between male and female secondary school students in their verbal scientific creativity. But no difference was found between the tribal and non-tribal students in verbal scientific creativity.

- A significant relationship between curiosity and scientific creativity was observed.
- Again, a significant relationship between divergent production abilities and mental imagery was found in the study.

Mukherjee M. (2007) has taken 250 students of class XI and XII of English medium school as sample for her study for Ph.D. degree titled "A study of Creativity in relation to Need-achievement, Manifest Anxiety and Level of Aspiration". She has found that boys do not differ from girls on the fluency, flexibility, originality and elaboration of both verbal and figural creativity.

Neelam (2008) in her study on 630 students of eleventh class studying in higher secondary schools of Jammu division concluded that positive significant correlations exist between home environment and emotional competency of students

On the relationships between creativity of children and environments (both School and Home), Richa Sharma (2011) has done a research work. The objectives of the study were:

1. To find the creativity level of government and private secondary school children.
2. To find the creativity level of boys and girls.
3. To find the difference in the creativity of children due to creative stimulation dimension, cognitive dimension and permissive dimension of school environment.
4. To find the creativity level of children with rich and poor home environment.

Sample: 200 students of class nine of Chandigarh were taken as sample and the sample were collected through random sampling. The sample comprised of 100 government school students (50 boys and 50 girls) and 100 private school students (50 boys and 50 girls).

Tools used: The following tools have been used in this study

1. Non-Verbal Test of Creative Thinking (Mehdi, 1985)
2. School Environment Inventory (Mishra, 1984)
3. Home Environment Inventory (Mishra, 1989)

Results

1. The school environment of government and private schools of Chandigarh did differ with respect to Creative Stimulation, Cognitive Encouragement and Permissiveness dimensions of school environment but did not differ significantly with respect to Rejection, Acceptance, and Controlled dimensions.
2. The government schools of Chandigarh provide greater creative stimulation to their students as compared to those studying in the private schools. Whereas in comparison with the government schools, private school students feel greater rejection.
3. As regards the comparison of creativity of the school students with their school environment, it can be concluded that the government schools of Chandigarh have higher creativity generating environment as compared to private schools of Chandigarh.

2.3 Researches on Creativity with Freedom

According to the Business Dictionary, 'Freedom' may be defined as the Right to express one's ideas and opinions freely through speech, writing, and other forms of communication but without deliberately causing harm to others' character and / or reputation by false or misleading statements.

Freedom asserts the opportunity which given for the exercise of one's powers, rights, desires or the like. Freedom consists two dimensions – in mind and expression. These are associated with one's thought and action of freedom.

Garnett (1960) mentioned in his speech in American Philosophical Association that in any list of the things of man value, especially in this twentieth century and on this side of the iron curtain, freedom is found to stand high. By many it would be mentioned as the first and most fundamental value in the life of man. Yet of its nature and conditions we are far from sure. By the term "creativity" I refer to a type of movement or change which is manifest only in living things, but is characteristic of them. It is productive of new form and order, of increasing variety or differentiation of form together with increasing elaboration and combination of forms, of increasing harmony, order and efficiency.

Children are born and brought up in the family and they are influenced by the family environment. They may get different degree of freedom in their thinking and different actions. Here, mainly parental child rearing practices are responsible for creating different levels of freedom. Nijhawan, H. K. (1972) used the test on Child Rearing Practices in her research study titled "Anxiety in School Children". She had selected High Anxious (HA) children and Low Anxious (LA) children from the sample of 720 students. She found that more parents of High Anxious (HA) children than of Low Anxious (LA) children favour the statements (structures towards, punishment, aggression, developing dependence) regarding parents' unquestionable authority over children, keeping children under strict discipline and beating the child for misconduct. They also believed that children should be helped in the little difficulties of life and that they should not hide anything from their parents. Mothers and fathers of HA children showed more discrepancy between their attitudes than those of LA children. Again, more of HA mothers used beating or rejection as a measure of disciplining the child than LA mothers. Fathers of LA children communicate with their children more than fathers of HA children.

Philip & Johnson (1988) in their study, "Freedom and Constrain in Creativity" mentioned some important statements.

1) Creativity is a mystery, and many people believe that it should remain a mystery. The anxious romantic says,

it should not be scrutinized too closely, because there lies a danger in knowing very much about it. If we discover its sources, they may dry up. The cynical realist asserts a different proposition.

2) The nature of free will for to be creative is to be free to choose among alternatives.

3) The problem of free will and the problem of creativity are, in some respects, one and the same. They can both be solved together.

4) We are free not because we are ignorant of the roots of many of our decisions, which we certainly are, but because we know that we can choose how to choose, and we know that among the range of options are those arbitrary methods that free us from the constraints of any ecological niche or any rational calculation of self-interest.

5) Creativity depends on arbitrary choices and thus on a mental device for producing, albeit imperfectly, non-determinism.

6) Creativity is like murder – both depend on motive, means and opportunity. On the creation of works of the imagination, society has dramatic effects.

7) Creativity yields products with three characteristic properties:

a) They are novel for the individual who creates them.

b) They reflect the individual's freedom of choice and accordingly are not constructed by rote or calculation, but by a non-deterministic process.

c) The choice is made from among options that are specified by criteria.

Olszewski-Kubilius (2001) mentioned in the study that the family creates an atmosphere where children are free to develop a unique identity and have their own individual thoughts and express them freely. Children who come from such type families are more competent and creative, in their work. Such families foster creativity and intellectual risk taking. The circumstances within homes and families that create environments conducive to the development of independent identities and thought are many and varied. For the reduction in parent-child identification they include anything, an "emotional space" between child and parent, less parental monitoring of children, and lower levels of conventional socialization of children by parents. In the literatures Circumstances cited which create this "space" include both positive and negative ones, such as difficult family or imbalanced parental relationships , as well as more benign, typical positive circumstances where parents are less related with children because they have careers or interests (Ochse, 1993; Olszewski-Kubilius, 1997). It is thought that in order to get autonomous, independent and less sex-stereotyped children these conditions help.

Murray, B. (2002) mentioned the statement of Dr. Teresa Amabile in the article, "A ticking clock means a creativity drop" in *American Psychological Association.* When the pressure's on, people produce—so the conventional wisdom goes. For making widgets hat may be true, but for producing creative ideas it's not the actual recipe, said social psychologist Teresa Amabile, Ph. D., the Edsel Bryant Ford Professor of Business Administration at Harvard Business School, in a 2002 APA Annual Convention talk. In her studies of creativity in corporate America, she has found that the more workers feel crunched, the less likely they are to solve a tricky problem, envision a new product line or have other such "aha!" experiences that qualify as innovation And workers don't tend to realize this, said Amabile, often assuming that the harder and longer they have worked, the more creative they have been. Time pressure quashes creativity, Amabile posits, because it limits people's freedom to ponder different options and directions. "Think of it as the way you might enter a maze and explore for a solution," she said. "With increased time pressure, you take the simplest pathway, not one that's elegant or creative. But if you're able to spend more time exploring the maze, you're more likely to hit on exciting or new solutions." That's the pattern Amabile found among 177 highly educated employees in seven U.S. chemical, high-tech and consumer-products companies.

Tibetan spiritual leader the Dalai Lama (2010) has stressed the need for individual freedom to ensure overall growth of human creativity in his address on "Human Rights Through Universal Responsibility" at the Assembly auditorium of Madhya Pradesh, India. According to Him, "Without freedom, one's creativity cannot bloom. Right to freedom is pivotal for the progress of any society. And for this, there should be a sense of global responsibility, a feeling of oneness for all beings".

Creativity is the freest form of self-expression. There is nothing more satisfying and fulfilling for children than to be able to express themselves openly and without judgement. The ability to be creative, to create anything from the personal experiences and feelings, can nurture and reflect children's emotional health. The experiences children have during their first years of life can significantly enhance the development of their creativity.

All children need to be truly creative is the freedom to commit themselves completely to the effort and make whatever activity they are doing their own. What's important in any creative act is the process of self-expression. Creative experiences sometimes help children to express and cope up with their feelings.

Children need plenty of opportunities for creative play and creative thinking. Activities should be given based on the children's interests and ideas.

Barker (2011) has given another view in his research study. According to him, Freedom is often associated with creativity, yet recent work in the decision making literature suggests that too much freedom can be paralyzing when it provides too many choices. In the study, a curvilinear effect of constraint on creativity was identified such that a moderate degree of constraint was more conducive to creativity than either a high or a low degree. The findings of the study suggest that while some amount of choice is important for encouraging creativity, too much can be counterproductive, which runs counter to many popular theories of creativity.

Kim (2011), Professor of Education at the College of William and Mary, analyzed scores on a battery of measures of creativity—called the Torrance Tests of Creative Thinking (TTCT)—collected from normative samples of schoolchildren in kindergarten through twelfth grade over several decades. According to Kim's analyses, the scores on these tests at all grade levels began to decline somewhere between 1984 and 1990 and have continued to decline ever since. The drops in scores are highly significant statistically and, in some cases, very large. In Kim's words, the data indicated that "children have become less emotionally expressive, less energetic, less talkative and verbally expressive, less humorous, less imaginative, less unconventional, less lively and passionate, less perceptive, less apt to connect seemingly irrelevant things, less synthesizing, and less likely to see things from a different angle." According to Kim's research, all aspects of creativity have declined, but the biggest decline is in the measure called Creative Elaboration, which assesses the ability to take a particular idea and expand on it in an interesting and novel way. Between 1984 and 2008, the average Elaboration score on the TTCT, for every age group from kindergarten through 12th grade, fell by more than 1 standard deviation. Stated differently, this means that more than 85% of children in 2008 scored lower on this measure than did the average child in 1984. Kim herself calls it the "creativity crisis,"

Creativity is nurtured by freedom and stifled by the continuous monitoring, evaluation, adult-direction, and pressure to conform that restrict children's lives today. In the real world few questions have one right answer, few problems have one right solution; that's why creativity is crucial to success in the real world. But more and more we are subjecting children to an educational system that assumes one right answer to every question and one correct solution to every problem, a system that punishes children (and their teachers too) for daring to try different routes.

"Paradoxically, creativity theories on the tension between freedom and constraints", says Brent Rosso (2011), an organizational psychology professor at Montana State University who studies the balance between freedom and constraint in the product development process. They are the yin and yang of creativity".

Jacobs T. (2013) mentioned the report of *Anna Steidle* in his article "Dim Lighting Sparks Creativity" in *Pacific Standard: The Science of Society*. "Darkness increases freedom from constraints, which in turn promotes creativity," report *Anna Steidle* of the University of Stuttgart and Lioba Werth of the University of Hohenheim. A dimly lit environment, they explain in the *Journal of Environmental Psychology,* "elicits a feeling of freedom, self-determination, and reduced inhibition," all of which encourage innovative thinking.

Steidle and Werth describe six experiments which provide evidence for their thesis. The key one featured 114 German undergraduates, who were seated in groups of two or three in a small room designed to simulate an office. The results is that those in the dimly lit room solved significantly more problems correctly than those in the brightly lit room. They also felt freer and less inhibited than their intensely illuminated counterparts. Participants in the bright and the conventionally lit rooms did not differ significantly from one another on either scale. "These results indicate that dim illumination' heightens perceived freedom from constraints, which in turn improves creative performance," the researchers concluded.

2.4 Researches on Creativity with Socioeconomic Status

According to Wikipedia, Socioeconomic status (SES) is an economic and sociological combined total measure of a person's work experience and of an individual's or family's economic and social position in relation to others, based on income, education, and occupation. When analyzing a family's SES, the household income, earners' education, and occupation are examined, as well as combined income, versus with an individual, when their own attributes are assessed.

Again, according to Mosby's Medical Dictionary, the definition of Socio-economic Status is the position of an individual on a social economic scale that measures such factors as education, income, type of occupation, place of residence, and, in some populations, heritage and religion.

Max Weber (1947) distinguishes between 'Class' and 'Status'. By class, he means a person's market situation, which depends mostly on whether he owns property or wealth. Market situation, he asserts, determines income and the life chances which depend on this. By status, Weber, means social honour and social esteem; and he believes that more acquisition of wealth is not by itself status groups. Thus, status is intricately related to some reputation, or prestige or so.

Chaplin (1928) defined Socio-economic Status as : Position an individual or a family occupies with reference to the prevailing average standards of cultural possessions, effective income, material possessions and participation in the group activities of the community.

For practical empirical purposes, Ogburn and Nimkoff (1972), suggested that a classification of population into social status groups based on occupation was most useful. They thought, occupation was closely related to income and education and to attitudes, beliefs and style of life.

In practice, SES of a family is determined on the basis of information about, location; type and conditions of dwelling house; nature of occupation; amount and source of income; education, material possession; cultural ecology of home – participations in social group, organization, recreational activities; extent of land owned, wealth etc., caste, religion etc.

Lichtewalner & Maxwell (1969) measured the creativity of 68 middle and lower-class Caucasian children attending a nursery school, kindergarten, or day-care centre by an object-identification originality test. The Mann-Whitney U test was employed to analyse differences, with a confidence level of 0.05. Firstborn and only children were significantly more creative than later-born children. Middle-class children were significantly more creative than lower-class children. It was concluded that enrolment in a pre-school programme alone is not sufficient to increase the creativity of lower-class children to the level of their middle-class peers.

Ogletree & Ujlaki (1973) conducted a creativity study in England, Scotland and Germany, which included 1,165 primary school children. Results showed that creativity scores (using the Torrance Tests of Creative Thinking) were a function of socio-economic background. In all countries, children of upper-class families obtained significantly higher creativity scores (verbal and non-verbal) than the children of middle- and lower-class families. The same significant difference was evident in middle class children to lower class children. This was true when analysed within countries, by age, grade and sex. There was no evidence to support the contention that youngsters of lower-class backgrounds performed better on non-verbal tasks than their higher-class peers, although they did make a better showing on the non-verbal tasks than on the verbal tasks.

Keenan & Victoria (1978) have done a research on creativity. They wished to determine the relationship between the sixth-grade student's creativity in art and certain socio-cultural and community factors.

A questionnaire was used to gather the socio-cultural information. A battery of three tests was used to determine each child's creativity in art. The instruments used were the Barron-Welsh Art Scale, the Paper Shapes, and Torrance's Test of Creative Thinking Figural Form A. The dependent variable in this study was a composite score of creativity derived from the scores of the individual tests.

Sample: The 340 students involved in this study were enrolled in the sixth grades of fourteen public elementary schools in North Texas and Central Texas during the 1968-69 school year.

Findings: An analysis of the data revealed there was no significant difference in the creativity of the sixth-grade student as a function of the size of the community in which he lived or his socio-economic group membership.

There was no significant difference in creativity of the three ethnic groups, Negro American, Latin American and Anglo-American, as evidenced by the composite score of creativity and the scores of the Paper shapes test and the Barron-Welsh Art Scale, Torrance's test indicated Anglo-American and Latin American students tended to have an advantage over Negro American students with regard to those factors (fluency, flexibility, originality and elaboration) which this test purports to measure. No relationship was found to exist between the student's creativity in art and maternal occupational status or church activity.

Miller & Gerard (1979) reviewed some research works and their opinions were stated as – "Family influences on the Development of Creativity in Children: An Integrative Review". Sample and measurement differences are considered in resolving discrepancies and integrating the findings. Social class is positively related to children's verbal creativity, but findings are mixed when nonverbal assessments are used. Younger children who are distant from sibs in age tend to be less creative. Other birth order findings are inconsistent. Gender differences in creativity are absent in most samples of very young children, but differences appear and widen developmentally, with older girls doing better on verbal tests and older boys on figural tests. Parents of creative children tend to feel personally secure and be highly competent. Relationships between creative children and their parents tend to be neither overly close emotionally, nor hostile and detached, but marked by respect, independence and freedom.

Biswas, P. C. (1988) has done a research titled, "Reactions to Frustration in School Children" for Ph. D. degree from Kalyani University. The sample was 904 students of High Schools, of Class VI, VIII, X where 424 boys and 480 girls in the sample. The findings were that SES has effect on types of aggression, directions of aggression and superego factors and patterns. He mentioned that the enriched learning and cultural environment fostered by the High and the Middle SES homes, presumably, have conditioned the children in such homes to grow comparatively mature and socialized at least in handling frustrating situations. However, more absolute study involving other related aspects of home environment, marital adjustment of parents, child rearing practices etc. and their interactions on the reactions to frustration elicited by adolescents, is required to gain better understanding of influence of S. E. S. on the dependent variable concerned.

Bradley & Corwyn (2011) believe that Socioeconomic Status (SES) remains a topic of great interest to those who study children's development. This interest derives from a belief that high SES families afford their children an array of services, goods, parental actions, and social connections that potentially redound to the benefit of children and a concern that many low SES children lack access to those same resources and experiences, thus putting them at risk for developmental problems. The interest in SES as a global construct persists despite evidence that there is wide variability in what children experience within every SES level, despite evidence that the link between SES and child well-being varies as a function of geography, culture, and recency of immigration, and despite evidence that the relation between SES and child well-being can be disrupted by catastrophes and internal strife .This Study provides an overview of the association between SES and children's well-being for three major domains of development(cognitive, socio-emotional, health).

Mankar *et al.* (2011) have done a research work titled "Creativity in children as function of parent occupation and socio-economic status" in *International Multidisciplinary Research Journal,* where they established the relationships among creativity, parent occupation and socioeconomic status. They think that creativity appears early in a life and its shows in the child's play. Gradually it spreads to other area of life. Studies of creative production of men and women, showed that creativity normally reaches its peak during the thirties and the either remain on a plateau of gradually declines. Some children are subjected to environmental factor that result in satisfying their creativity at these periods while other children of the same age are not.

The attempts were made in the present investigation to correlate the creativity in children with their parent occupation and socio-economic status, as it was assumed parent in good financial condition can adequately satisfy the need of children to enhance their creativity. Creative thinking was also considered their different occupation, have different effect on family life and creativity of children.

The investigation was carried out at various schools in Akola. Children ranging from 10 to 15 year were also tested on socioeconomic status scale. For measuring creativity of the student and socioeconomic status of parents, the standardized creative thinking test by Mehdi (1973) and socioeconomic status scale by Rajeev Bharadwaj (1980) were administered respectively.

Surprisingly the result of present investigation explain that socio-economic status and occupation of parent are showing insignificant correlation with the creativity of children (r=0.03833). There is no impact of parent occupation on their children's creativity (r=0.05158). The figure shows negative and insignificant correlation. Hence concluded that creativity is an independent phenomenon, which is not related with any occupation or availability of material things. Creativity is a potential and can developed through positive reinforcement & motivation in children.

Venu Gopal Rao & Satyapal (2011) have found out some results from their research work. According to them, creativity comes out when Mind, Heart and Hand (Action) work together, mind is store of idea and takes interest to act on the ideas. Physical Body is store of energy, mind is store of ideas and heart is store of emotions. It means "Ideas + emotion + energy = creativity. Creativity is ability to create or invent something new and original ability to solve problem. The creativity is an ability to recognize how the best process of developing new, rare or unique ideas. Creativity is an ability to distinguish how the best practice and unusual ideas can be applied in different situations.

Sample: A sample of 300 students studying at Post Graduation level in different academic streams has been gathered. While picking the respondents due care has been taken to make the sample representative of the universe of the study.

Results

- There is significant difference in the flexibility dimension language creativity of male and female. Male performed better than female. It means gender play an important role to expose creative potential.
- There is significant difference in the flexibility dimension of language creativity of Rural and Urban. Urban performed better than Rural. Thus, residence affects the creative ability of individual.
- There is significant difference in the flexibility dimension of language creativity of type of families (Nuclear and Joint). Nuclear Family students performed better than Joint.
- There is no significant difference in the flexibility dimension of language creativity on mother occupation (H. W. and in-service).
- There is significant difference among scheduled caste students on father occupation on Flexibility Dimension of Creativity. Those students are more creative whose fathers are businessmen than whose fathers are in private job, government job and laborers.
- There is significant difference among scheduled caste students on Family income, on Flexibility Dimension of Creativity. High income families' students performed better than lower income families.

Saha (2012) has done a research work titled "Creativity in relation to Socio-economic Status in Secondary School Students in West Bengal" where he wished to provide information and relation between creativity and socio-economic status in West

Bengal, India. Data were collected through TTCT for creativity and socio-economic status scale of Kuppuswamy of 100 secondary students of Birbhum District in West Bengal, by randomly. The result revealed that 1) Creativity is positively related with socio-economic status, 2) boys and girls students do not differ significantly in their creativity, 3) boys and girls students are not differ with regard to socio-economic status.

According to Niwas and Punia (2013), Creativity is journey of human being's dissatisfaction to satisfaction. Every creative work is a reflection of human mind and aesthetic sense. Aesthetic sense is related with beauty. Beauty of world depends upon beauty of mind because every beautiful creation is product of mind and mind does so when it feels dissatisfaction and hunger to find something new, highly creative people can do this type of task. The survey method was used in this study. 300 post graduate schedule caste students were considered as a sample. The sample was selected randomly. The data were analysed using mean, SD, t-test and F-test. The findings of the study were (1) there is highly significant difference in scientific creativity (fluency, flexibility and originality) of male and female, rural and urban, SCI and SC2. There positive relationship is found among parent's occupation, parent's education, family income, academic stream and scientific creativity.

Parsasirat *et. al.* (2013) found out the relationship between Socioeconomic Status and Creativity in their study titled, "Effect of Socioeconomic Status on Emersion Adolescent Creativity" in *Asian Social Science.* In this study family economic status, father's education and mother's education were the three dimensions of socioeconomic status. This exploratory correlational research study examined the relationship between family economic status, father's education and mother's education with adolescent creativity. The sampling method was employed to select the proportion of participants using stratified and multi-stage cluster random sampling. The population of the sample was 546 high school students in Education Region 4, Tehran. The participants, 249 males and 297 females, completed two questionnaires. The adolescents completed a Demographic Characteristics

Questionnaire and Abedi Creativity Questionnaire, which were used as the measuring tools in this study. The results show a significant positive correlation between family economic status and creativity ($p < .01$), and between parent education and creativity ($p < .01$). Interestingly, the analyses revealed a strongly significant positive correlation between parent education and creativity ($p < .01$), although none was found between males and females on creativity.

2.5 Conclusion

In reviewing related literatures, the present researcher found that some studies highlighted socio-economic status along with other influencing factors of the family on creativity of the children. Some researchers have stressed on parental behaviour, the relationship between creativity and academic achievement of the children. Most of the studies have dealt with gender difference in creativity. But, in this point, different results were found in different research studies. No one study was found considering the socio-economic status of the family along with the important factor- freedom of thought and actions enjoyed by the children in the family.

3

METHODOLOGY AND DESIGN

This chapter had been divided into three parts, the first part was devoted to the methodology, the second part described the tools used in the study and the third part dealt with the general procedure.

PART - I

3.1 Nature of the Study

The main approach of this study was survey. But this survey was done through several tests and questionnaires in a particular field area to collect the valuable data. Hence, it was field survey. This study aimed at finding out the abilities of the target groups and to determine relationships between dependent variable (Creativity) and independent variables (Freedom of the Students, Socio-economic Status, Gender). For this purpose, scores were calculated on the basis of performances or responses of the sample students in the given tests and questionnaires. So, it was obviously a quantitative research which described some relationships among the concerned variables. Hence, this study was a field survey descriptive research quantitative in nature.

3.2 Methodology

The main purpose of the study was to determine the relationship between criterion (Creativity) and predictor variables (Freedom, Socio-economic Status, Family Tension, Family Structure). For this purpose, the descriptive survey method of educational research had been followed. In this study the researcher performed the investigation on pupils of secondary level (grade VIII and IX).

Collected data were arranged according to their code numbers. The magnitude of the relationship was determined by the researcher personally through the use of the coefficient of correlation with the help of computer software SPSS version 12.0. Besides this, graphical representation helped to describe the relationship clearly.

Inferential Statistics - analysis of variance (ANOVA), t-test had been applied to compare the ability between Boys and Girls, or between the groups - High and Low of each independent variable (Autonomic and Syncratic co-operative for Family Structure). The inferential statistics helps the researcher to test the hypotheses and to get some important inferences.

Multiple regression is one of the most frequently used technique of analysing data in behavioural research. It is a method of analysing the collective and separate contributions of two or more independent variables (Predictor variable) to the variation of a dependent variable (the criterion). In this case, the co-variation between a set of independent variables with the dependent variable was being considered.

The important aim of multiple regression analysis is prediction. In this research, one of the major objectives was to know to what extent creativity could be predicted on the basis of Freedom, Socio-economic status and Family Tension.

3.3 Population

All the students of grade VIII and IX of Bengali medium schools under West Bengal Board of Secondary Education, of two districts Nadia and North 24 Parganas were the population of this study. So, the students studying in class VIII and IX at English or Hindi medium schools under West Bengal Board of Secondary Education or any other Board of Education were not considered in this population. Also, the schools run by the private bodies were not included in the target population. Different versatile characteristics were found in the families of these two districts due to Geographical position, Cultivation, Industrial growth, Handicrafts, Education, Medical facilities, Political effects and nearer to the metropolitan city-Kolkata.

As the diversified families lived in these two districts, so variety types of students, with respect to their family environment, might be found in the population.

3.4 Sample

The sample consisted of 372 school going students of class VIII and class IX from eight different types of schools of district Nadia and North 24 Parganas. All the selected schools were of Bengali Medium under West Bengal Board of Secondary Education. There were 179 boys and 193 girls in the sample. Different types of schools were selected randomly from the both districts- according to a particular ratio.

The intellectual development and functioning take a very sophisticated shape at Formal Operation Stage (Piaget,1952) as the child learns to deal with abstraction by logical thinking. Here the child, age of 11 and above, learns to utilize the tool of symbolism as effectively as possible in the process of thought and problem solving. He begins to construct relationships between concrete operations and between symbols. He also begins to look at problems in many ways and explore various solutions but in a very systematic and logical way. Keeping this aspect in mind, the investigator selected the students of class VIII and class IX as the sample for this study.

3.5 Sampling Frame and Sampling Techniques

Total 372 students of class VIII and class IX were taken as the sample for this study. They were selected from different types of schools of different places of the two districts. Sampling frame of this study was as follows:

Table – 3.1: Showing the Number of Selected Schools for Sample

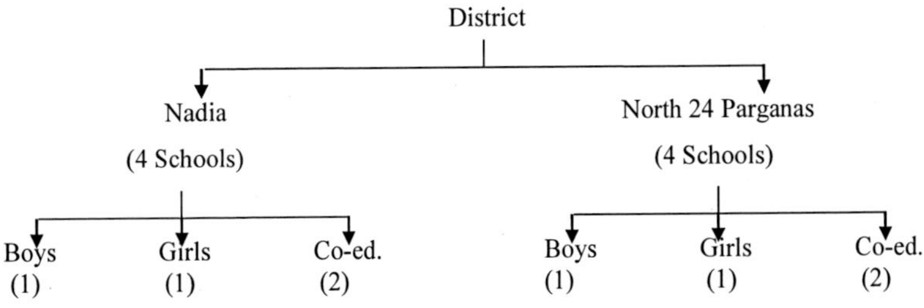

Table – 3.2: Showing the Sample Size

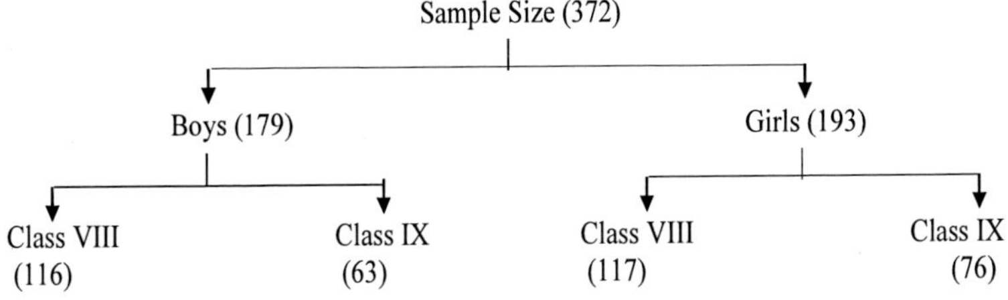

For selecting the sample, stratified random sampling technique was used. The process of sampling was done as follows:

Step – I: The researcher first prepared a list of Bengali medium secondary and higher secondary schools under West Bengal Board of Secondary Education for the two districts – Nadia and North 24 Parganas separately.

Step – II: From the above-mentioned list, three types of schools, viz.; Boys' school, Girls' school and Co-educational school, were separated and thereby three lists of schools were obtained for each district.

Step – III: It was found that the number of such type of Boys' school was 70 and the number of Girls' school was 86 and the number of Co-educational schools was 235 in Nadia district. Similarly, in the district of North 24 Parganas, the number of Boys' school was 195 and the number of Girls' school was 224 and the number of Co-educational schools was 401. All the schools were arranged serially under the particular category where a particular school contained a particular serial number.

Table – 3.3: Showing Description of the Sample

Code No.	Name of the Schools and Place	Type	District	Grade–VIII		Grade–IX		Total
				Boys	Girls	Boys	Girls	
1	Dhanicha High School (H. S.), Chakdaha	Co-ed.	Nadia	15	14	15	18	62
2	Shantipur Oriental Academy, Shantipur	Boys	Nadia	29	–	28	–	57
3	Shaktinagar Girls' High School, Krishnagar	Girls	Nadia	–	18	–	24	42
4	Belgharia High School, Belgharia	Boys	24 Pgs. (N)	15	–	11	–	26
5	Khantura Girls' High School, Gobardanga	Girls	24 Pgs. (N)	–	28	–	17	45
6	Deshbandhu High School, Naihati	Co-ed	24 Pgs. (N)	31	27	09	17	84
7	Kataganj Gokulpur Adarsha Shikshaniketan, Gayeshpur	Co-ed	Nadia	22	23	–	–	45
8	Pearah Teghoria High School (H. S.), Baduria, Basirhat	Co-ed	24 Pgs. (N)	04	07	–	–	11
	Total	116	117	63	76	372		

Step – IV: Out of total 8 schools, 4 schools were selected from each district. Again, out of 4 schools, one Boys' school, one Girls' school and two Co-educational schools were selected. The researcher drew at random the serial numbers of one Boy's school, one Girls' school and two Co-educational schools from each district by using lottery technique.

Both districts had diversified areas which included part of A-I city, several Municipalities, Industrial Organisations, Business Markets, many villages and cultivated lands. So, the inhabitants of these areas, no doubt, were very different in profession as well as in family conditions. Therefore, the students who came from these families, treated as sample, might be of different degree of components of family environment. Hence, the description of the sample given in Table 3.3 would provide a perfect representation of the population of the study.

3.6 Variables

The main objectives of the study were: to identify the creative individuals, gender difference in components of creativity, relationships between components of creativity and different aspects of family environment. Thus, the variables for this study were as follows:

A) Independent Variables:

Independent variables in this study were as follows:

i) Freedom of thought and actions enjoyed by the students in the family,

ii) Socio-economic Status of the family,

iii) Gender.

B) Dependent Variables:

Dependent variables in this study were students' performance scores, only on three components of creativity, obtained from verbal and non-verbal creativity tests.

i) Fluency (verbal fluency, non-verbal creativity).

ii) Flexibility (verbal flexibility, non-verbal flexibility).

iii) Originality (verbal originality, non-verbal originality).

3.7 Sources of Data

The required data were collected from the sample by using different tools and techniques. Near about 800 students of class VIII and class IX of 8 different types of schools of district Nadia and North 24 Parganas (4 schools from each district) had been assigned for the sample. Out of 800 students only 410 students were present in all the tests held on two conjugative days. Again, out of 410, some students were irresponsible, careless or unable to follow the instructions of the tests and some concealed true information. Ultimately 372 students (179 boys and 193 girls) were as the sample of the study from where data were collected.

PART – II

3.8 Tools Used

The following tools were used in the present study:

3.8.1 Sarker's Creativity Tests

Sarker's Creativity Tests were developed by Sarker, A. K. (1994) and could be administered to individuals at all educational levels above six years of age. The tests consisted of several batteries of test activities – verbal and non-verbal form. Both the verbal and non-verbal tests of activities assessed the products in terms of fluency, flexibility and originality.

Sarker's Creativity Test was a standardized test prepared by Sarker, on the scores of the students of Bengali medium schools of West Bengal. These test batteries had three forms:

1) Long Form of Creativity Test.

2) Short Form of Creativity Test.

3) Intermediate Form of Creativity Test.

The Intermediate Form of Creativity Test had been chosen by the researcher for this present study considering different relevant situations. In administration of the tests, ***Sarker*** emphasized on the matter that the subjects would be understood about how to play the game, by giving an example about the test before commencement of the test. A certain time period was allotted for the particular test items.

The brief descriptions of the tests were given below:

3.8.1.1 Sarker's Verbal Test of Creativity

The verbal activities used as different games in the present study were as follows:

Game – 1: Unusual Uses

The unusual uses test using verbal stimuli were direct modification of Gilford's Brick Uses Test. Here three tasks were given to the subjects to write down their unusual uses. That three tasks were 'Tin cans', 'Newspaper' and 'Brick'. Below the every task item, there was a space for their responses. There was 6 minutes of time period to write down the unusual uses.

Game – 2: Similarity Task

There were two task items to find out the similarities between two components or products. These similarities would be exceptional from common similarities. The two task items were "water and air" and "shoe and cap". Space was given below each task item, so that the students could response point wise. There was 5 minutes time to respond.

Game – 3: Consequences Tasks

There were 2 impossible situations and the subjects were asked to find out the new, uncommon and different responses as the results of the situations in the long run within 5 minutes of time. The subjects would write down the responses in the blank spaces provided below of each of the items.

Game – 4: Common Problem Tasks

This task was an adaptation of Guilford's (1951) test designed to assess the ability to see defects, needs, deficiencies and found to be one of the tests of the factor termed "sensitivity to problems". Two common problems raised in daily life were given in this game. The subjects were asked to write down new and uncommon different problems or difficulties as many as possible within 6 minutes of time. Space was provided below each of the tasks to write down their responses.

Game – 5: Product Improvement Tasks

The Improvement tasks were adapted from Guilford's (1952) Apparatus Test which was designed to assess ability to see any kind of defects, an aspect of sensitivity to problems. In these tasks, two products were given and the subjects were asked to think of as many improvements as they can within 8 minutes time.

3.8.1.2 Sarker's Non-verbal Test of Creativity

There were 4 tasks selected in Non-verbal Test of Creativity for this present study. These were as follows:

Game – 1: Circle Test

The circle task was originally designed as a non-verbal test of ideational fluency and flexibility. The directions were then modified in such a way to stress originality and elaboration. This task to stress originality and elaboration. This task consisted of 30 small circles (one-inch diameter). The subjects were asked to use the circles as the main part of the objects which they would sketch.

The objects would be variety of types and uncommon as far as possible within 12 minutes time. Fluency, Flexibility and Originality were encouraged by the instructions and test records were scored for each of these three components.

Game – 2: Incomplete Figure Tasks

Incomplete Figures task was an adaptation of the Drawing Completion Test, developed by ***Barron (1958)***. The incomplete figures techniques had also been used in a variety of psychological tests for other purposes. An incomplete figure was set up before an individual and asked him to complete it as in the simplest and easiest way as possible. Thus, to produce an original response, the subjects usually had to control his tensions and delay gratification of this impulse to closure. In this game, there were six incomplete figures in six rectangles of a page. The subjects might draw any picture or figure using each of the incomplete figure within total 8 minutes time.

Game – 3(A): Asking Questions Task

In this game, a picture of social situation was given to the subjects. How the subjects had curiosity, interest and awareness about the social environment and how far they thought about the situation were the objectives of this test. Their responses must be in question form about the situation in the picture within 5 minutes time. The subjects were encouraged by the instructions to have fluency, flexibility and originality in their responses. The test records were scored for these three components.

Game – 3(B): Asking Questions Task

In this game, the subjects were asked to respond in question form about the real product of daily use. Here, a watch was shown before them for one minute and they were allowed to ask questions about the whole watch, its different parts, its functions etc. within 5 minutes time. Questions as responses were scored for fluency, flexibility and originality.

Scoring

The scoring procedure in the present study was the same as given in the test manual and scoring guide (1994). All the responses were scored for fluency, flexibility and originality. The fluency score was obtained by counting the number of different relevant responses. At first, the relevant responses were sorted by striking off the irrelevant responses. Then the relevant responses were categorized as per scoring guidance laid down in the scoring manual. Flexibility score was determined by counting the number of category changes. Originality was determined on the basis of statistical infrequency of responses as laid down in the scoring manual of the test. On the basis of that *criterion*, weightages were assigned to all the probable responses or types of responses. Thus, each response was given a value. The Originality score was determined, for that respondent, by adding up the values or weightages of all responses.

The manual strictly described that the raw scores of fluency, flexibility and originality should not be added up because each variable had a different mean and different standard deviation. Thus, the raw scores for fluency, flexibility and originality had been converted into standard scores. For convenience in handling the scores and omission in the negative signs of the standard scores, the raw scores had been converted into T-scores (M =50; SD = 10). Total Fluency had been determined by adding up of fluency of verbal creativity and that of non-verbal creativity after converting each of them into T-scores. Similarly, Total Flexibility and Total Originality were calculated only for Regression Analysis in the present study.

Reliability

Although most of the usual concept of reliability were relevant to the assessment of creativity, the very nature of this ability was to create a number of problems in interpreting reliability data. Most of the theories of creative functioning emphasized the significance of emotional factors, bodily stages, group atmosphere and family environment and the like. There were some like **Gordon (1961)** who insisted that "in the creative process emotional component is more important than the intellectual, the irrational is more important than the rational". Another difficulty in this context was that the life experiences of an individual might help or hinder creative functioning. Environment, emotional, physical, motivational and mental health factors also might affect creative development and functioning which made lower the test-retest reliability. In a number of test-retest reliability studies, as reported by *Torrance* (1966), reliability co-efficient were generally found higher for fluency and flexibility than for originality. However, these results were not confirmed in another study (*Dalbec*, 1966) who obtained test-retest reliability co-efficient of 0.59 for fluency, 0.35 for flexibility, and 0.73 for originality over a four years period.

In Sarker's Creativity Test, for different test items of both verbal creativity and non-verbal creativity, coefficients of reliability for test-retest were ranging from 0.73 to 0.92. Again, the co-efficient of reliability for different test items of both verbal and non-verbal creativity by split-half method were ranging from 0.68 to 0.88.

Validity

A person can behave creatively in an almost infinite number of ways. Therefore, according to *Torrance*, it would be ridiculous even to try to develop a comprehensive battery of tests of creative thinking that would sample any universe of creative thinking abilities. *Torrance* did not believe that any one could specify the number and range of test tasks necessary to give a complete assessment of a person's potentialities for creative behaviour.

Sarker's Creativity Test was reported to have high construct validity. This test tasks were standardized over the Bengalee school going students. Also, these tests were used in several Ph. D. research works (Sarkar, P.,1994; Biswas, P. C., 1988).

3.8.2 Sarker's Freedom Test

Sarker (1986) developed a Freedom Test for school going children in Bengali, and it was standardized on the students of Bengali medium schools of West Bengal. Freedom of thought and actions in the family and in the school might foster the creative potential in the children. The test items concerned with the freedom of thought and work in scientific experiments, hobby, personal views or in daily life style. There were 29 test items out of which 25 items were about thought and actions in the family and only 4 items were about that in school. There were three options – 'True'; '?'; 'False' put against each of the statements. The correct response was done by underline one out of the three options according to the student's view.

Scoring

According to freedom of thought and actions, the correct response against each of the statements was given in test manual. The percentage of freedom was calculated as follows:

$$\text{The Freedom Index} = \frac{\Sigma F}{N} \times 100$$

where F = correct response for Freedom and N = the total number of test items. In the present study the investigator calculated Freedom score by adding up Fs, the correct responses for freedom, as the score would describe the respondent in the relative placement.

Reliability

Reliability of the test was reported to be very satisfactory. The co-efficient of reliability for test-retest was 0.78.

Validity

The validity index of this test was 0.63.

3.8.3 Sarker's Socio-economic Status Test

Standardized Tests of Socio-economic Status provide numerical description of the family and home in the context of social hierarchy. *Chapin's* (1988) scale had been widely used by the social researchers for assessing Socio-economic Status on the basis of various criteria of home and family, such as, income, occupation, the number and condition of household or living room articles, membership in social and cultural organizations extent of wealth possessed by the family.

In India, *Kuppuswamy* (1962) devised a Socio-economic Status scale (for urban area) which included three categories of items: education, occupation and income. Weightages were assigned to seven items for each category. This scale was reported to be highly reliable and valid and had been widely used in the Hindi belt of India.

Pareek and Trivedi (1964) developed a Socio-economic Status Scale (for rural area) in which the criteria of Socio-economic Status were: occupation, education, social participation of the head of the family, caste, land owned, house type, farm powers, material possessions and general nature of the family. This scale had been widely used in Hindi belt of India, where it was standardized.

Sarker (1998) developed a single Socio-economic Status scale for the urban, industrial and rural children in Bengali and it was standardized on the high school children of West Bengal. This scale was latest revised in the year 2007 on the high school children of Bengali medium school of West Bengal. It included the following major items: *education, profession, income of parents, extent of land owned, house (own or rented), condition of house, subscription of newspaper and periodicals, musical instruments and possession of household materials (their quality and numbers)*. The chief contention of ***Sarker*** was that, information given by children regarding parental income, educational qualification and profession, land owned by the family can hardly be reliable but children could easily supply reliable information regarding articles possessed by the family; hence, he paid more emphasis on the information of children regarding possession of articles in assessing Socio-economic Status.

Scoring

The items of the scale were scored by assigning weights according to the directions written by ***Sarker*** in the manual.

Reliability

Test-retest reliability of the scale was 0.95 which was significant beyond 0.01 level. Split-Half reliability of the scale was 0.87.

Validity

Co-efficient of correlation between the scores for the scale and data obtained through actual home visit was 0.86 which was reported to be significant at 0.01 level.

Again, correlation between the scores of ***Sarker's*** scale and that of ***Kuppuswamy*** and ***Pareek and Trivedi*** on the same sample, were very high (above 0.9 in each case).

Norms

The following criteria were used to classify different strata – High, Middle and Low:

High Socio-economic Status Group → Top 27% of the scores,

Middle Socio-economic Status Group → Middle 46% of the scores,

Low Socio-economic Status Group → Lower 27% of the scores.

The ***Sarker's*** Socio-economic Status scale was used in this study for the following reasons:

i) It was standardized over the same type of sample as was used for this study.

ii) It was simple and easy to score.

iii) Language used in the tool was Bengali.

iv) Its norms had recently been established.

v) Reliability and validity of this scale was found satisfactory.

vi) This single tool could be utilized for the rural, industrial and urban areas.

PART – III

3.9 Procedure

For the purpose of collecting data, rapport was established with the students by explaining them the objectives of the study in brief. The data were collected by administering the tests in normal classroom situation. The total time taken for collection of data was 20 weeks.

The sequence of tests administration in each of the 8 schools was as follows:

Day	Class	Test Administered
Day – I (First Half)	VIII	Sarker's Creativity Tests (Verbal and Non-verbal)
Day – I (Second Half)	IX	Sarker's Freedom Test, Sarker's Socio-economic Status Test
Day – II (First Half)	IX	Sarker's Creativity Tests (Verbal and Non-verbal)
Day – II (Second Half)	VIII	Sarker's Freedom Test, Sarker's Socio-economic Status Test

While administering the tests selected in this study, the following instructions were given to the students:

3.9.1 Administration of Sarker's Creativity Test

Before passing out the booklets, the following brief orientation instructions were given to the students in the classroom setting, which would make a particular group to be honest, arouse interest and motivate for performance.

"I believe you will have lot of fun doing the activities we have planned for. This test will give you a chance to see how you are at thinking up new ideas and solving problems. The test will call for all imagination and thinking ability you have. So, I hope that you will put on your best thinking and you will enjoy yourself".

At this point the booklets were given to the students and they were asked for giving the identification information on the front page. Moreover, the following information was given to the students in Bengali in the classroom:

"All the activities are arranged here as different games of different types in the two booklets. Out of two booklets, one (Verbal Form) is already given to you. It contains 5 games and each of the games has its particular rules and regulations to play it. The other booklet (Non-verbal Form) contains 3 games to play. These games will give you a chance to use your imagination in thinking up ideas and putting them in the form of words and pictures. There are not any right or wrong answers in the games. Try to think of as many ideas as possible which are interesting and unusual within particular time period. Work as fast as you can. Write the answers in simple and concise. Don't worry about the bad hand writing and spelling mistakes. Figures need not to be much clear and fair. If you run out of ideas before time is called, wait until next instructions are given. If there is any difficulty after the start, raise your hand, I will help you".

3.9.1.1 Creativity Test (Verbal Form)

Game – 1: Unusual Uses Tasks

Instruction

"In this game, there are 3 different materials in your sheet. Your duty is to write down as many as possible different unusual uses of each product

at the blank space below within 6 minutes time. Uses should be of different types. Remember that the products may be small or big in size or any other form as you like".

An example was given with a piece of cloth. The unusual uses of a cloth were discussed among the subjects and the investigator to make understand about their activities.

"You should write down that uses which are really cheerful, cleverest, uncommon, unthinkable to your peers and different in nature. As the time is very short, only 6 minutes, your responses should be very simple and concise and you should not think about the spelling mistake in the responses".

To measure the time duration a stop watch was used. After the due time, the page was turned over rapidly.

Game – 2: Similarity Tasks

Instruction

"In this game, you have a page containing the names of two pairs of materials. You should have to find out the new and uncommon different similarities between the two materials as many as possible within 5 minutes time".

An example was given with the pair – "Train and Tractor". The subjects tried to find out the similarities with the help of the investigator. Investigator also mentioned some cheerful, cleverest and uncommon similarities.

"You should try to find out that similarities which are unique and very new and what your peers can not think yet. Your responses should be very simple and concise and you should not think about the spelling mistake in the responses".

To measure the time duration a stop watch was used. At last the page was turned over shortly after the time over.

Game – 3: Consequences Tasks

Instruction

"In this game, you have the page containing 2 impossible situations. You should have to find out the new, uncommon and different responses

as the results in the long run of that impossible situation within 5 minutes of time".

An example was given to the students with the impossible situation – "What would happen, if all the houses were floating in the sky'. The students tried to find out that responses with the help of the investigator. Investigator also added some uncommon and new responses about that impossible situation.

"I think you have understood about the game. You should write down that results which are really new and uncommon and what your peers can not think yet. Mind that your responses should be of different types. As the time is short, only 5 minutes, your responses should be simple and concise. Do not think about the spelling mistake in your responses".

A stop watch was used to measure the time duration. When the allotted time was over, the page was turned out rapidly.

Game – 4: Common Problem Tasks

Introduction

"In this game, you have the page containing two common problems raised in your daily life. You should have written down new and uncommon different problems or difficulties as many as possible within 6 minutes of time".

An example was given to the student with – "What problems raise in taking a bath". Subjects were tried to find out the problems in connection with the situation.

"You should write down that unique and uncommon problems, what your peers can not think yet. You should mention as many problems as you think that might arise in connection with these situations. Do not think about the spelling mistake in your responses".

Allotted time period was measured with the help of a stop watch. When the time was over, the page was turned over rapidly.

Game – 5: Product Improvement Tasks

Introduction

"In this game, you have the page containing the names of two common products. You should suggest as many ways as you can to improve these products within 8 minutes of time".

An example was given to the subjects with "the clay made doll". Subjects were tried to give some suggestions to improve the doll with the help of the investigator.

"You should mention that suggestions which make the product more interesting, attractive, workable and useable. Do not worry about whether or not it is possible to make this change. You should write down that new and uncommon changes what your peers can not think yet. Do not think about the spelling mistake in your responses".

Allotted time period was measured with the help of a stop watch. When the allotted time was over, the sheet was collected rapidly.

3.9.1.2 Creativity Test (Non-verbal Form)

The second booklets were distributed among the students. After giving their information on the first page, the subjects were instructed to turn over.

Game – 1: Circle Task

"In this game, you have the page which contains 30 circles of 1inch diameter each, your duty is to draw various pictures or objects as many as possible by adding lines within 12 minutes time. The circles should be the main part of whatever you make. You can place marks in the circles, outside the circles or both sides of the circles – Whenever you need to complete the picture. Try to think of things that no one else will think and make as many different pictures or objects as you can and put as many ideas as you can think. Add name or title below each of the objects".

As example, the investigator draws 9 objects in the Black Board by using triangles given early. After due time, the page was turned over soon.

Game – 2: Incomplete Figure Task

Introduction

"In this page, there are 6 rectangles which contain 6 incomplete figures, one in each rectangle. You should sketch some interesting objects or pictures by adding lines to the incomplete figures on this page within 8 minutes

time. Try to think of some picture or object that no one else will think in your class. Do not stop with your first idea for completing the figure; keep building onto it. Make up an interesting title or name for each of the figure at the bottom of the block".

After due time, the page was turned over soon.

Game – 3(A): Asking Questions Task

Instruction

"The main objective of this game is to know how far you are interested and curious about the social environment where you live. You have already got the page containing a picture of a social situation at the top of the page. Try to write down as many as possible questions which arise in your mind linked with the situation within 5 minutes time. These questions may be related with the fact, part of the picture, whole picture, the past and future happen. Avoid the questions whose answers may be obtained by seeing the picture. The questions must be related with the picture and must express your interest and curiosity. But the questions should be very different with respect to subject-matter, meaning and sequence. Make an interesting name or title of the picture at the bottom of the block".

Allotted time is measured by a stop watch and after completion of time, the paper was turned over rapidly.

Game – 3(B): Asking Questions Task

Instruction

"This game is as like as the earlier one. You should make questions about a product of daily use as many possible as you can within 5 minutes time. A wrist watch will be shown before you for a one minute. You should write down the related questions about part of the watch, whole watch, its functions, its structure, its manufacturing etc. as many possible as you can. Write down that questions which no one else can think of. Mind it, you will write down that questions whose answers are not available by seeing the watch. Besides these, the questions must be simple, precise and different in nature. Mention an interesting name of the watch.

After completion the allotted time, the booklets were collected from the students rapidly.

3.9.2 Administration of Sarker's Freedom Test

Freedom Test was the first test for administration on the second day of data collection. After distributing the Test sheets among the students, they were instructed to write down their identifying information in the space given at the top of the sheet.

Instruction

"There are 29 test items in your booklet which has already given to you. There are three options – ***'True'****;* ***'?'****;* ***'False'*** *put against each of the statements. If you think the statement is true for you, then underline* ***'True'*** *and is false for you, then underline* ***'False'****. If the statement is not true and not false or do not understand the statement, then underline the question mark* **(?)**. *You have no time limit to respond. Your responses will be highly concealed and nobody will know it. Moreover, it will be used only for this study".*

After completion, all the sheets were collected in the class.

3.9.3 Administration of Sarker's Socio-economic Status Test

Socio-economic Status Test was the second test for administration in the second conjugative day of data collection. The researcher tried to make rapport with the students by describing the objectives of the tests, ensuring about the concealment of data and explaining the importance of this work.

Instruction

"You have already got a questionnaire sheet titled "Socio-economic Status Test". You should respond what actually exists in your family. You should write down your parents' qualification, occupation and monthly income at the spaces given therein. You should also write down, so far correct, own land property, different rooms in house, newspaper etc. and on the next page, give a tick (ü) mark which good is existed in your family and give a cross (´X) mark which does not exist in your family. Also, mention the quantity of goods within bracket. You have no fixed time limit to respond. Remember that your responses will be highly concealed and nobody will know it. Moreover, it will be used only for this study.

After completion of the answers, the answer sheets and the question booklets were collected in the class.

3.10 Data Collection

The tools and techniques, mentioned early, had been used for the collection of data. All the tools had been administered personally by the investigator as it was thought appropriate on account of the complexity of the tests, its instructions and to maintain uniformity in the testing procedure.

All the tools were administered to all the students of that classroom to avoid unexpected situations in the hall. The tools were administered in two conjugative days in the same classroom. Some students were absent either of the two days, i.e., they were not present in all the tests. Moreover, some were irresponsible, careless or unable to follow the instructions of administration of the tests and some concealed true information. Ultimately 372 students out of 800 students of class VIII and class IX were as the sample of the study. Scoring of the responses of the total sample had been done in accordance with the scoring procedures mentioned in the test manuals. These scores were treated as the raw data for the present study, which had been later converted into T-scores only for Regression Analysis. The data thus obtained had been systematically tabulated with their code for analysis and interpretation.

3.11 Statistical Method

The collected data from the sample were subjected to different statistical techniques. All the statistics used in the study can be divided into four major parts as follows:

A) Descriptive Statistics

B) Inferential Statistics

C) Correlational Statistics, and

D) Multiple Regression Analysis

A) Descriptive Statistics

In order to find out the nature of sampling distribution, descriptive statistics were carried out for each variable. For this purpose, the statistics such as Range, Minimum, Maximum, Mean, S. D., Skewness, Kurtosis were calculated with the help of Computer Software SPSS–12.0. Moreover, pie-graphs were plotted in somewhere to describe the groups.

B) Inferential Statistics

One-way ANOVA design was adopted to find out whether there was any significant mean difference between boys and girls or high and low groups under consideration.

After ensuring about the significance of the mean difference between two groups, 't'-test had been applied to know the difference in two means, the higher group in details.

C) Correlational Statistics

Testing the relationships among the variables of the present study, multiple correlation method was applied. For this purpose, Pearson's Product Moment method was used. The correlation index had been calculated among independent variables – Freedom, Socio-economic Status and dependent variables – Fluency, Flexibility, Originality of both verbal and non-verbal creativity. Apart from these, partial correlations were also calculated for each independent variable to assess the impact of the individual independent variable on the dependent variables (components of creativity – Fluency, Flexibility and Originality).

D) Multiple Regression Analysis

Multiple Regression model was used in the present study to predict the impact of three independent variables, i.e.; Freedom, Socio-economic Status on the dependent variables. The model was developed separately for three components of creativity (both verbal and non-verbal together) – Total Fluency, Total Flexibility and Total Originality. These were symbolized as Y and Freedom, Socio-economic Status were symbolized as X_1, X_2 respectively. In the present study the used Multiple Regression Equation was as follows:

$$\hat{Y} = a + \beta_1 x_1 + \beta_2 x_2$$

where 'a' was constant and β_1 β_2 were the relative weights. Beta weight (β-weight) was calculated to determine the relative importance of the independent variable. In other words, β weight would tell the amount of change in the dependent variable as a result of a standardized change in one of the independent variables controlling for all other independent variables using a common unit of measurement.

Thus, in this study, components of creativity might be predicted from a linear combination of Freedom (of thought and action enjoyed by the students in the family), Socio-economic Status, Family Tension. The -value analysis had been done for each of the Multiple Regression Equations.

3.12 Level of Significance

All the hypotheses in this study were tested on the basis of the results obtained through the analysis of the data using the statistical methods mentioned early. In comparison between the two groups on a particular variable being investigated or relationships among the variables, the hypotheses were tested at 0.01 and 0.05 level of significance. As the data analysis was done by using computer software SPSS -12.0, the 'F'-values, 't'-values or 'r' etc. were found with their respective level of significance directly. The researcher had interpreted the results of analysis by considering 0.01 and 0.05 level of significance only.

4

PRESENTATION, ANALYSIS AND INTERPRETATION OF DATA

This chapter had been devoted to the presentation of data, analysis of it and interpretation of the results based on the analysis of data collected. This chapter mentioned its different parts with different considerations, such as, Part-I: Organization of Data, Part-II: Descriptive Statistics, Part-III: Graphical Representation, Part - IV: Inferential Statistics and Part-V: Correlational Techniques & Regression Analysis.

PART - I

ORGANIZATION OF DATA

4.1 Presentation of data in tabular form

By using different tools, the collected data were arranged in a tabular form according to the CODE number. All the scores were put under the category of tests viz., Verbal Creativity (Fluency, Flexibility, Originality), Non-verbal Creativity (Fluency, Flexibility, Originality) and the tests of different independent variables viz., Freedom, Family Structure, Socio-economic Status and Family Tension.

The following six digits code had been used for a particular set of data obtained from a particular student:

Class	Gender	School	Roll No.	Section
*	*	*	**	*

Class: VIII 1→IX →2

Gender: Boy →1, Girl → 2

School

Dhanicha High School (co-ed.), Chakdaha, Nadia →1

Shantipur Oriental Academy (Boys'), Shantipur, Nadia →2

Shaktinagar Girls' High School (Girls'), Krishnagar, Nadia → 3

Belgharia High School (Boys'), Belgharia, 24 Pgs.(N) → 4

Khantura Girls' High School (Girls), Gobardanga, 24 Pgs.(N) →5

Deshbandhu High School (Co-ed.), Naihati, 24 Pgs. (N) →6

Kataganj Gokulpur Adarsha Shikshaniketan (co-ed.), Gayeshpur, Nadia →7

Pearah Teghoria High School (co-ed.), Baduria, Basirhat, 24 Pgs. (N) → 8

Roll No.: Same as class Roll No. stated in the questionnaire by the student.

Section: Same as stated by the student in the questionnaire like A / B / C / D.

Table 4.1.1: Scores of all the Students of the Sample under the Study

SL. No	Code	Verbal Creativity			Non Verbal Creativity			Fd	SES
		Fu	Fx	Or	Fu	Fx	Or		
1	11102A	44	26	54	23	13	47	20	99
2	11107A	38	18	45	9	1	8	6	30
3	11110A	45	29	40	22	6	23	8	44
4	11114A	34	15	47	25	15	24	19	79
5	11115A	32	21	49	21	10	26	15	106
6	11125A	33	14	24	21	10	22	19	67
7	11126A	29	16	32	24	5	26	13	91
8	11127A	24	12	26	8	1	7	15	63
9	11131A	35	17	32	21	8	22	16	89
10	11136A	37	24	48	17	9	10	16	34
11	11143A	29	13	24	24	17	22	14	62
12	11149A	33	19	36	18	8	12	17	51
13	11158A	15	4	16	19	13	16	18	81
14	11159A	24	12	29	15	10	10	18	37

Table 4.1.1: Contd...

SL. No	Code	Verbal Creativity Fu	Fx	Or	Non Verbal Creativity Fu	Fx	Or	Fd	SES
15	11160A	25	11	44	22	9	14	18	30
16	11201A	44	27	51	32	20	44	18	136
17	11202A	35	22	44	20	12	18	19	111
18	11203A	39	23	51	27	17	29	18	77
19	11204B	25	9	22	26	14	21	10	54
20	11205A	41	24	40	26	15	16	16	41
21	11205B	24	10	17	23	15	27	21	47
22	11207A	25	12	21	18	13	16	13	53
23	11209A	32	14	29	26	16	28	16	82
24	11210A	34	15	32	32	17	30	11	140
25	11217A	28	16	24	21	11	24	12	75
26	11218A	32	15	29	27	11	31	9	75
27	11220B	30	14	24	20	10	15	12	75
28	11222A	24	4	14	32	18	33	14	92
29	11223B	17	3	7	26	18	25	8	50
30	11224B	35	17	39	24	14	22	19	66
31	11226B	26	6	18	19	6	14	15	92
32	11228A	27	12	32	27	15	24	9	120
33	11237A	18	3	12	17	11	11	16	108
34	11239A	31	13	29	19	10	20	15	89
35	11243A	31	12	36	19	12	24	18	85
36	11244A	20	6	19	24	12	22	17	46
37	11254A	19	5	13	19	12	17	12	97
38	11257A	15	4	10	20	10	15	16	107
39	11272B	22	5	17	17	6	16	11	35
40	11282B	19	8	15	16	8	19	16	58
41	11287B	33	19	29	28	17	29	12	63
42	11294B	39	24	41	20	11	15	22	86
43	11296B	27	12	21	21	13	22	15	89
44	11297B	16	5	16	20	12	22	13	83
45	11401A	43	21	49	36	29	52	22	193
46	11402A	38	20	37	37	18	37	22	170
47	11404A	31	13	36	32	18	31	22	118
48	11407A	41	20	50	27	17	38	21	94
49	11408A	34	19	34	45	26	57	22	126
50	11409A	20	7	21	21	13	24	5	173

* Scores of all the students of the sample under study are given in Appendix-A

Notations used

Fu = Fluency, Fx = Flexibility, Or = Originality, Fd = Freedom, SES = Socio-economic Status of the family.

The above table contained the data of Creativity (verbal and non-verbal) in the dimensions of Fluency, Flexibility and Originality along with Freedom, Socio-economic Status of 372 students out of which 179 students were boys and 193 students were girls of both class VIII and class IX of different schools.

4.1.1 Statistical Techniques

In the present study, the obtained scores on different variables as warranted by the design of the investigation were studied. All the data were put and analysed by the researcher personally with the help of computer using SPSS - 12.0 Windows Version package and Microsoft Excel 2007.

In order to reduce the number of Multiple Regression Analysis, Total Fluency, Total Flexibility and Total Originality had been considered. Here, Total Fluency was calculated by adding Fluency of verbal creativity and Fluency of non-verbal creativity after transforming them into normalized standard score (T-score) separately. In the same way, Total Flexibility and Total Originality were calculated. These T-scores had been given in the Appendix - A. The employed statistics were:

i) Descriptive Statistics.

ii) Inferential Statistics.

iii) Correlational Techniques.

iv) Regression Analysis.

PART - II

DESCRIPTIVE STATISTICS

4.2 Descriptive Statistics of Dimensions of Creativity and Independent Variables

This part represented the analysis and interpretation by means of Descriptive Statistics by taking into consideration the scores of the Dependent Variables and the different Independent Variables.

Table 4.2.1: Descriptive Statistics of Dependent Variables for Boys

Sl. No.	*Dimensions of creativity*	*N*	*Range*	*Mini-mum*	*Maxi-mum*	*Mean*	*SD*	*Ske-wness*	*Kurt-tosis*
1.	Fu_V.C	179	43	9	52	30.88	8.885	.018	-0.400
2	Fu_N.V.C	179	41	8	49	27.13	7.126	.303	0.350
3	Fx_V.C	179	29	2	31	14.89	6.601	.046	-0.371
4	Fx_N.V.C	179	30	1	31	14.87	5.248	.328	0.660
5	Or_V.C	179	50	7	57	31.44	11.165	-.031	-0.734
6	Or_N.V.C	179	54	3	57	26.66	10.289	.679	0.474

Table 4.2.1 showed the Range, Mean, S. D., Skewness and Kurtosis of all the dimensions viz., Fluency, Flexibility, Originality of both verbal and non-verbal creativity as obtained by boys.

Table 4.2.2: Descriptive Statistics of Independent Variables for Boys

Sl. No.	*Independent variable*	*N*	*Range*	*Mini-mum*	*Maxi-mum*	*Mean*	*SD*	*Ske-wness*	*Kurt-tosis*
1	Freedom	179	21	5	26	15.59	3.990	-.125	-.269
2	S.E.Status	179	184	9	193	73.16	32.447	.818	.893

Table 4.2.2 showed the Range, Mean, S. D., Skewness and Kurtosis of all the Independent Variables viz., Freedom and Socio-economic Status; as obtained by boys.

Table 4.2.3 showed the Range, Mean, S. D., Skewness and Kurtosis of all the dimensions viz., Fluency, Flexibility, Originality of both verbal and non-verbal creativity as obtained by girls.

Table 4.2.3: Descriptive Statistics of Dependent Variables for Girls

Sl. No.	*Dimensions of creativity*	*N*	*Range*	*Mini- mum*	*Maxi- mum*	*Mean*	*SD*	*Ske- wness*	*Kurt- tosis*
1.	Fu_V.C	193	47	12	59	32.38	8.146	0.345	0.621
2	Fu_N.V.C	193	35	10	45	26.06	6.754	0.145	-0.144
3	Fx_V.C	193	42	1	43	16.41	6.913	0.891	1.674
4	Fx_N.V.C	193	25	4	29	13.45	4.731	0.239	-0.267
5	Or_V.C	193	75	6	81	33.71	12.656	0.840	1.820
6	Or_N.V.C	193	57	6	63	26.71	10.251	0.722	0.776

Table 4.2.4: Descriptive Statistics of Independent Variables for Girls

Sl. No.	*Independent variable*	*N*	*Range*	*Mini- mum*	*Maxi- mum*	*Mean*	*SD*	*Ske- wness*	*Kurt- tosis*
1	Freedom	193	18	7	25	15.90	3.853	0.246	-0.317
2	S.E.Status	193	172	16	188	82.82	36.216	0.290	-0.239

Table 4.2.4 showed the Range, Mean, S. D., Skewness and Kurtosis of all the Independent Variables viz., Freedom and Socio-economic Status; as obtained by girls.

Table 4.2.5: Descriptive Statistics of Dependent Variables for all Students

Sl. No.	*Dimensions of creativity*	*N*	*Range*	*Mini- mum*	*Maxi- mum*	*Mean*	*SD*	*Ske- wness*	*Kurt- tosis*
1.	Fu_V.C	372	50	9	59	31.66	8.531	0.141	0.097
2	Fu_N.V.C	372	41	8	49	2658	6.947	0.237	0.140
3	Fx_V.C	372	42	1	43	15.68	6.798	0.518	0.948
4	Fx_N.V.C	372	30	1	31	14.13	5.031	0.323	0.327
5	Or_V.C	372	75	6	81	32.62	12.000	0.531	1.110
6	Or_N.V.C	372	60	3	63	26.69	10.256	0.699	0.605

Table 4.2.5 showed the Range, Mean, S. D., Skewness and Kurtosis of all the dimensions viz., Fluency, Flexibility, Originality of both verbal and non-verbal creativity as obtained by all the students (boys and girls).

Table 4.2.6: Descriptive Statistics of Independent Variables for all Students

Sl. No.	*Independent variable*	*N*	*Range*	*Mini-mum*	*Maxi-mum*	*Mean*	*SD*	*Ske-wness*	*Kurt-tosis*
1	Freedom	372	21	5	26	15.75	3.917	0.053	-0.272
2	S. E. Status	372	184	9	193	78.17	34.746	0.532	0.100

Table 4.2.6 showed the Range, Mean, S. D., Skewness and Kurtosis of all the Independent Variables viz., Freedom and Socio-economic Status; as obtained by all the students (boys and girls).

PART - III

GRAPHICAL REPRESENTATION OF DATA

The raw data had been represented graphically for visual comparison of the percentage, spread, shape and slope of the distribution of the raw scores in different ways. Description of each graph might clarify the nature of the distribution and also its implications for this investigation.

4.3 Pie-graph for different groups

Table 4.3.1: Frequencies of Boys Groups for Each Independent Variable

Group	*Frequency*	*Percent*	*Cumulative Percent*
High	49	27.4	27.4
Low	49	27.4	54.7
Medium	81	45.3	100.0
Total	179	100.0	

The below pie-graph represented the three group of Boys for each Independent Variable (Viz.; Freedom, Socio-economic Status). Each of High and Low group contained 49 frequency separated from the Medium group of 81 frequency on the basis of 27% statistical rule. This was also showed in the Table 4.6.1.

Fig. 4.3.1: Pie Graph of Groups of Boys for Each Independent Variable

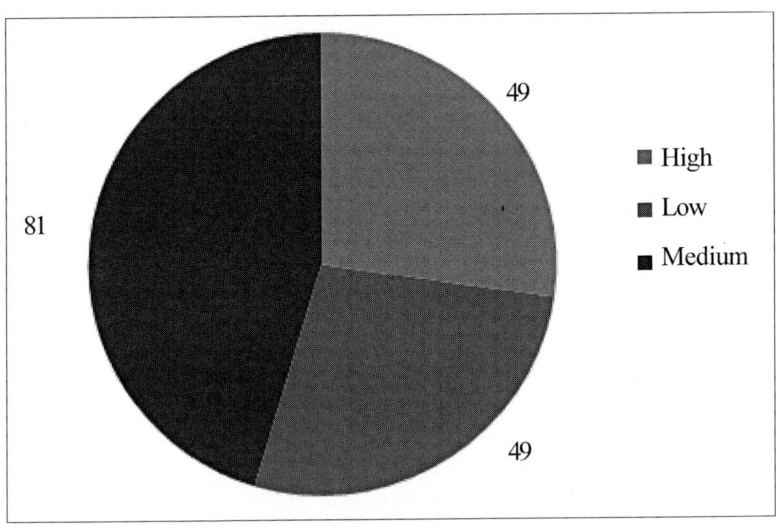

Table 4.3.2: Frequencies of Girls Groups for Each Independent Variable

Group	*Frequency*	*Percent*	*Cumulative Percent*
High	52	26.9	26.9
Low	52	26.9	53.9
Medium	89	46.1	100.0
Total	193	100.0	

Fig. 4.3.2: Pie Graph of Groups of Girls for Each Independent Variable

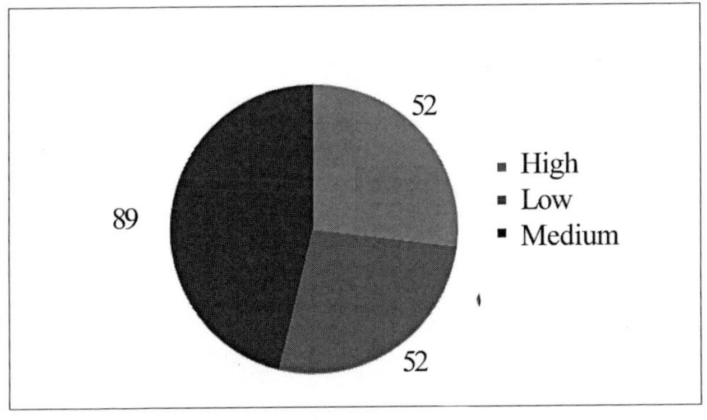

The above pie-graph represented the three group of Girls for each Independent Variable (Viz.; Freedom, Socio-economic Status). Each of High and Low group contained 52 frequency separated from the Medium group of 89 frequency on the basis of 27% statistical rule. This was also showed in the Table - 4.6.1.

Table - 4.3.3: Frequencies- of Groups of All Students (N = 372)

Group	Frequency	Percent	Cumulative Percent
High	100	26.9	`26.9
Low	100	26.9	53.8
Medium	172	46.2	100.0
Total	372	100.0	

Fig. 4.3.3: Pie Graph of Frequencies of Groups All Students (N = 372)

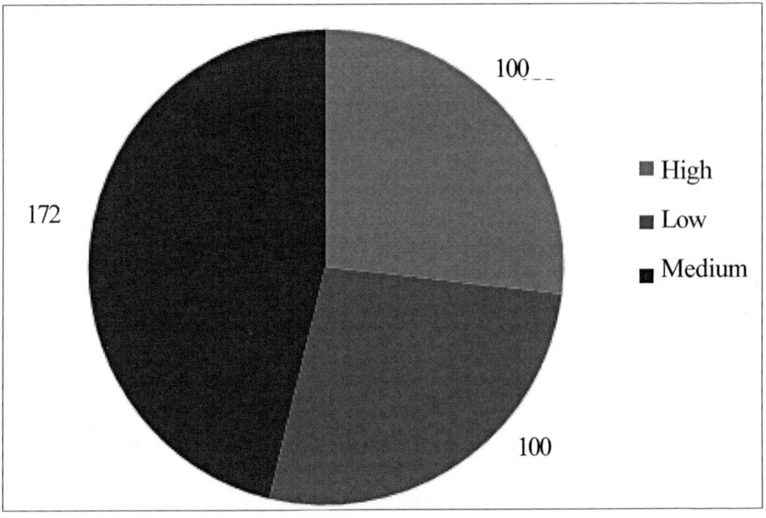

The above pie-graph represented the three groups (High, Low and Medium of all the students (N = 372) for each of the Independent Variables (viz. Freedom, Socio-economic Status). Each of High and Low group contained 100 frequency separated from the Medium group of 172 frequency on the basis of 27% statistical rule.

4.4 Ogive for Dimension of Creativity with Gender Difference

A useful overall comparison of two or more groups is provided when Ogives representing their scores on a given test are plotted upon the same co-ordinate axes. In this study, Ogives were plotted on the basis of scores obtained by 179 Boys and 193 Girls in Fluency, Flexibility, Originality of both verbal and non-verbal creativity tests. These graphical representations might clarify the comparison between the two groups - Boys and Girls in different dimensions of Creativity.

Fig. 4.4.1: Graphical Representation of the Distribution of the Fluency Scores in Verbal Creativity Test obtained by the Boys and Girls on the Same Axes

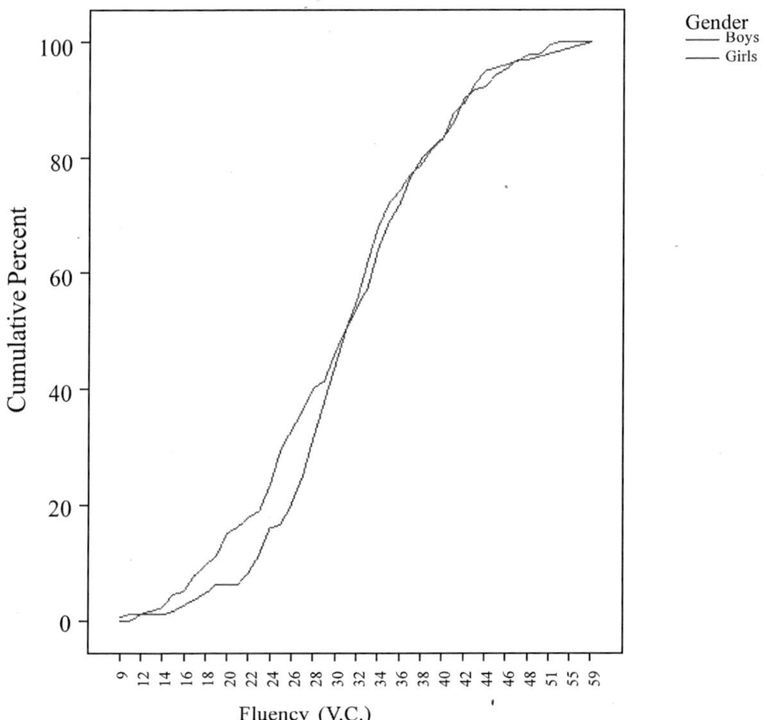

The above graphs described the comparison between the two groups - Boys and Girls in Fluency of Verbal Creativity. The girls' Ogive lay to the right of the boys' upto almost 75% of cumulative frequency. This indicated that point, the girls scores were consistently higher than the boys. Differences in ability as between the two groups were shown by the distances separating the two curves at various levels. At the very low scoring and the high scoring boys and girls were not different in Fluency of Verbal Creativity. The medians of the two groups were almost same.

Fig. 4.4.2: Graphical Representation of the Distribution of the Fluency Scores in Non-verbal Creativity Test obtained by the Boys and Girls on the Same Axes

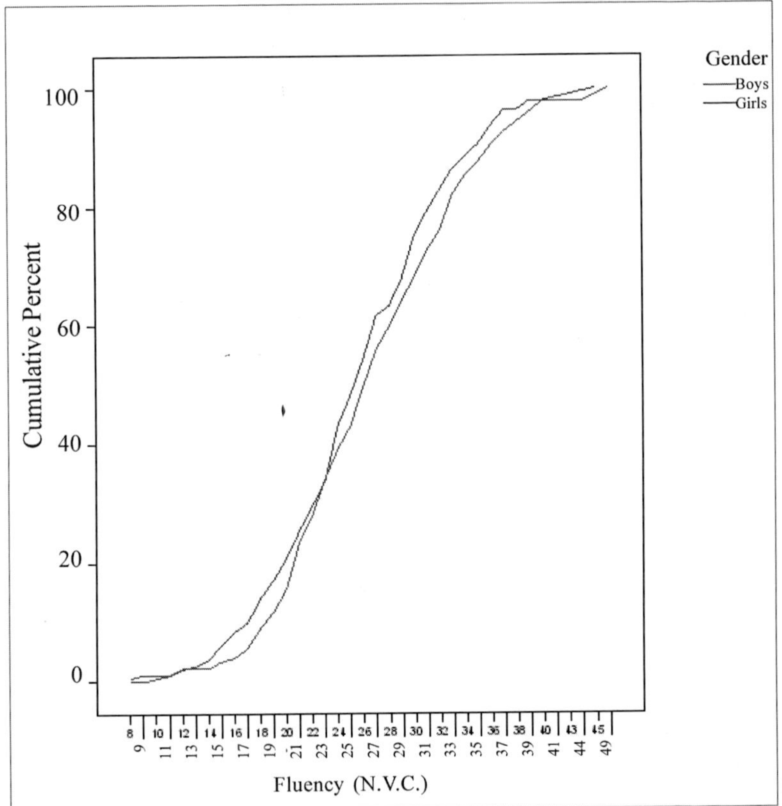

The above figures described the comparison between Boys and Girls groups in Fluency of non-verbal creativity. The boys' ogive lay to the right of the girls' over the entire range. It indicated that the boys scores were consistently higher than the girls. The separating distances at various levels indicated the differences in Fluency scores between the two groups. But at the extremes and at almost 30% of cumulative frequency, scores of Fluency (N.V.C.) of the two groups - Boys and Girls, were not so different.

Fig. 4.4.3: Graphical Representation of the Distribution of the Flexibility Scores in Verbal Creativity Test obtained by the Boys and Girls on the Same Axes

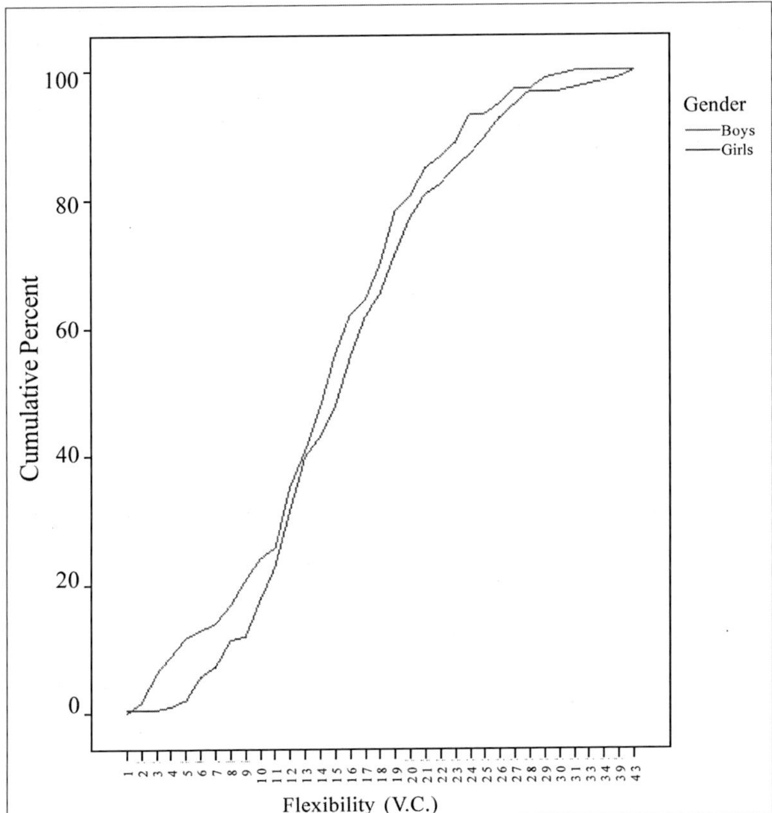

The above graphs showed the visual comparison between the two groups - Boys and Girls in Flexibility of Verbal Creativity. The girls' ogive lay to the right of the boys' over the entire range. It indicated that the girls scores were consistently higher than the boys. But at the two extremes and at about 40% level, the two curves met each other. At that levels boys' scores and girls' scores in

Flexibility (V.C.) were not so different. The separating distances between the two curves indicated the differences in scores of the two groups.

Fig. 4.4.4: Graphical Representation of the Distribution of the Flexibility Scores in Non-verbal Creativity Test obtained by the Boys and Girls on the Same Axes

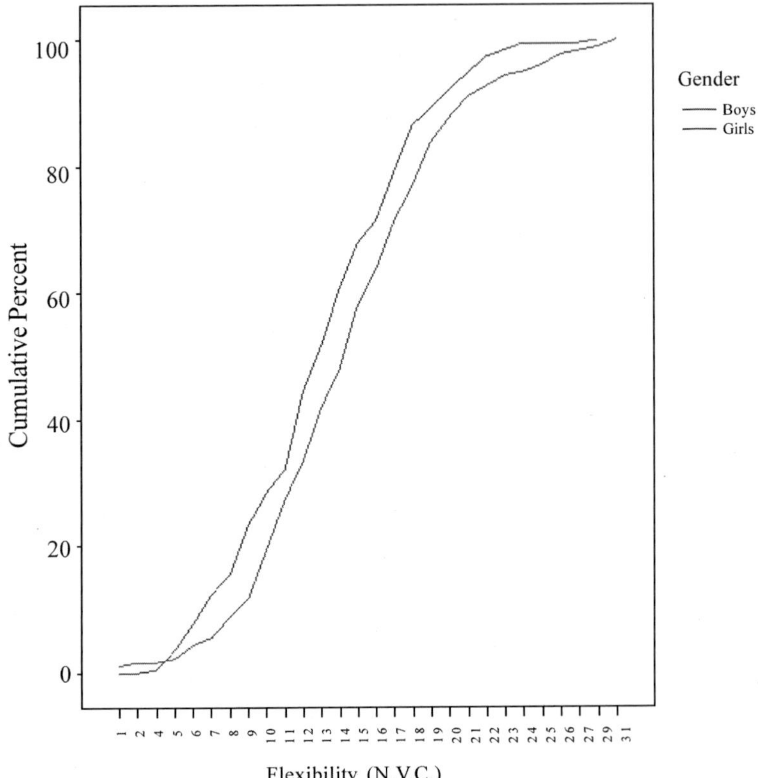

The above figures clearly showed the comparison between boys and girls groups in Flexibility of non-verbal creativity. Here, the boys' ogive lay to the right of the girls' over the entire range very distinctly. It indicated that the boys' scores were consistently higher than the girls. The separating distances which were almost same at various levels indicated the differences in Flexibility (Non-verbal Creativity) scores between the two groups. Only the differences at the very low scoring boys and girls were not so great. The medians of the two groups would be also different.

Fig. 4.4.5: Graphical Representation of the Distribution of the Originality Scores in Verbal Creativity Test obtained by the Boys and Girls on the Same Axes

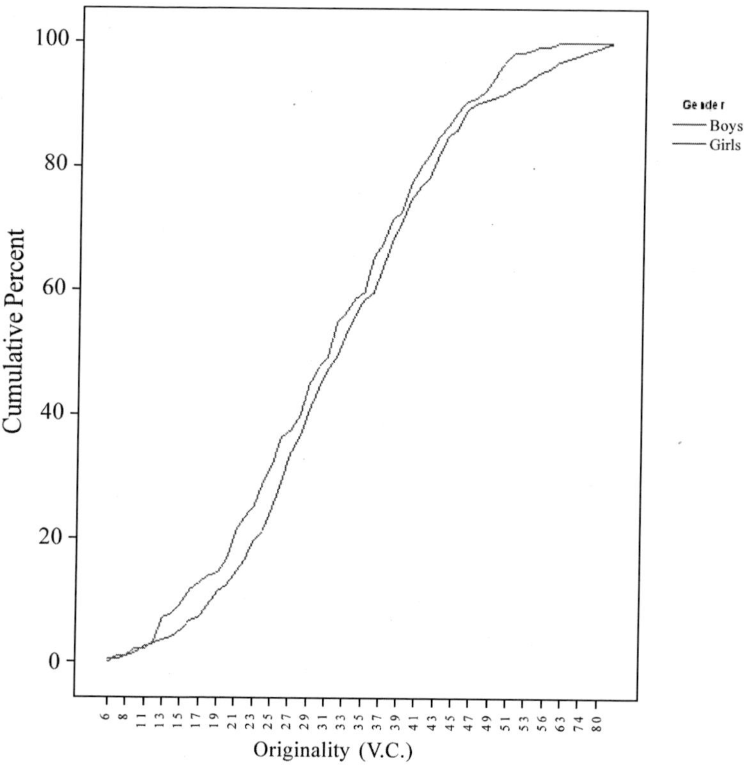

The above graphs showed the comparison between the two groups - Boys and Girls in Originality of Verbal Creativity. Here, the girls' ogive lay to the right of the boys' over the entire range. This indicated that the girls scores were higher than the boys at various levels. The separating distances between the curves indicated the differences in Originality (Verbal Creativity) scores of the two groups. But the distances at various levels were not uniform and at the two extremes points the ogives met each other. That meant, the very high scoring and the very low scoring boys and girls had no difference in Originality (V.C.) score.

Fig. 4.4.6: Graphical Representation of the Distribution of the Originality Scores in Non-verbal Creativity Test obtained by the Boys and Girls on the Same Axes

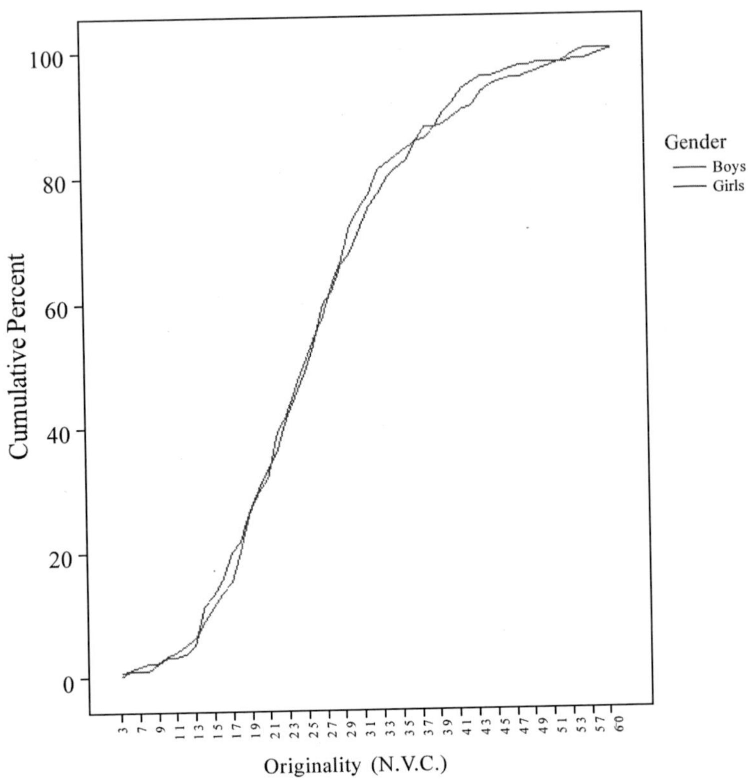

The above graphs showed the comparison between Boys' group and Girls' group in Originality of Non-verbal Creativity. Here, the ogives of boys' group and girls' group almost overlapped on each other. This indicated that the differences between the two groups, in Originality (Non-verbal Creativity) scores were not so great. That meant, there would be no difference between boys and girls in Originality of Non-verbal Creativity.

4.5 Graphical Representation of Dimension of Creativity and Independent Variables

In order to have a comparative study between the two groups - Boys and Girls, Multi-Line graphs had been plotted by calculating the mean scores of Fluency, Flexibility and Originality (for both Verbal and Non-verbal Creativity) with accordance to their class intervals of different independent variables, viz.; Freedom and Socio-economic Status. A pair of Line graphs described how the dimension of Creativity changed with the increase of the independent variable for Boys and Girls on the same axes. Naturally, the Mid points of class intervals of Independent Variables were put along X-axis and Mean scores of the dimension of Creativity (Dependent Variable) were put along Y-axis.

Table 4.5.1: Mean Scores of Fluency and Class Intervals of Freedom

Freedom Class Interval	*Mid-point of Class Interval*	*Mean Verbal Fluency*		*Mean Non-verbal Fluency*	
		Boys	*Girls*	*Boys*	*Girls*
6 - 10	8	27.28	31.50	24.86	26.78
11 - 15	13	29.39	31.12	26.63	24.50
16 - 20	18	31.60	33.39	27.09	27.34
21 - 25	23	36.78	34.04	31.22	26.95

Fig. 4.5.1.1: Graphical Representation of Mean Fluency Scores in Verbal Creativity Test with Freedom for Boys and Girls on the Same Axes

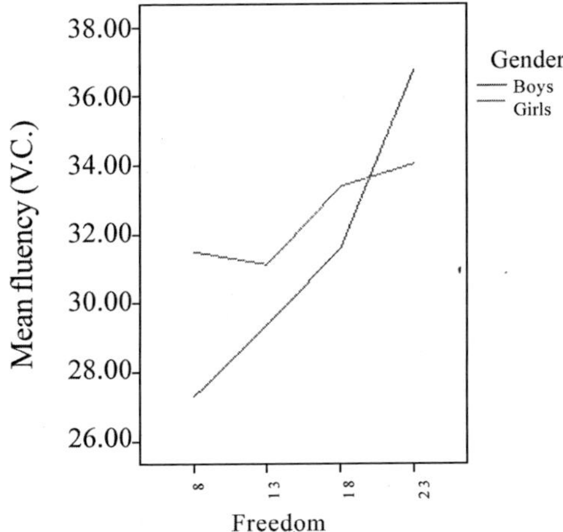

Fig. 4.5.1.2: Graphical Representation of Mean Fluency Scores in Non-verbal Creativity Test with Family Freedom for Boys and Girls on the Same Axes

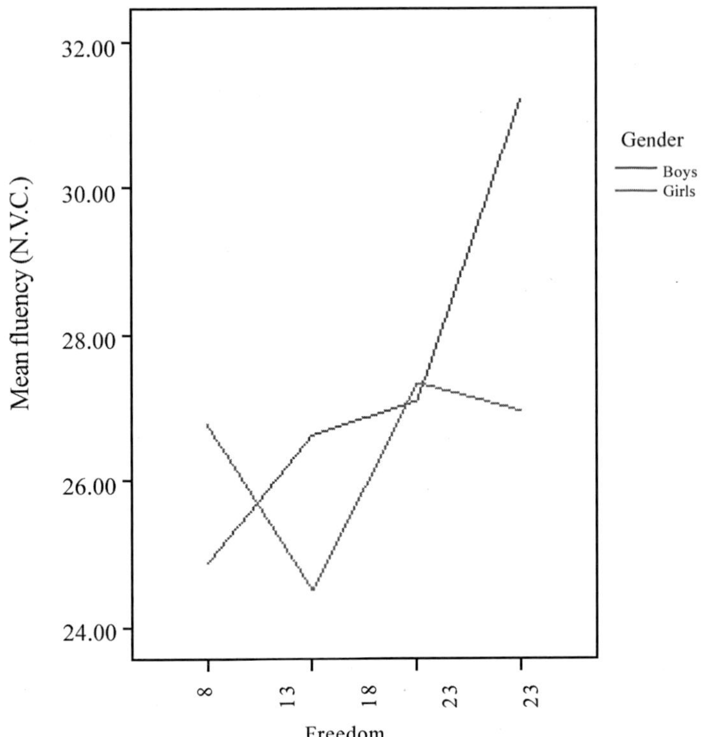

The relationship between Fluency and Freedom was visually represented by the Figure 4.5.1.1 and Figure 4.5.1.2 for verbal and non-verbal creativity respectively for the two groups - Boys and Girls. Here, Fluency increased gradually with increase of Freedom for both girls and boys. Boys' obtained Fluency scores were always greater than girls' in the Figure 4.5.1.2. But, in Figure 4.5.1.1, girls' scores were greater than boys', though, the highest scores contained the boys. Abnormally, girls' Fluency scores decreased at the middle part of Freedom in the Figure 4.5.1.2.

Table 4.5.2: Mean Scores of Flexibility and Class Intervals of Freedom

Freedom Class Interval	*Mid-point of Class Interval*	*Mean Verbal Fluency*		*Mean Non-verbal Fluency*	
		Boys	*Girls*	*Boys*	*Girls*
6 - 10	8	13.57	16	13.52	13.71
11 - 15	13	13.36	15.02	14.07	12.71
16 - 20	18	15.47	17.68	15.30	14.01
21 - 25	23	18.78	17.43	17.17	14.00

Fig. 4.5.2.1: Graphical Representation of Mean Flexibility Scores in Verbal Creativity Test with Freedom for Boys and Girls on the Same Axes

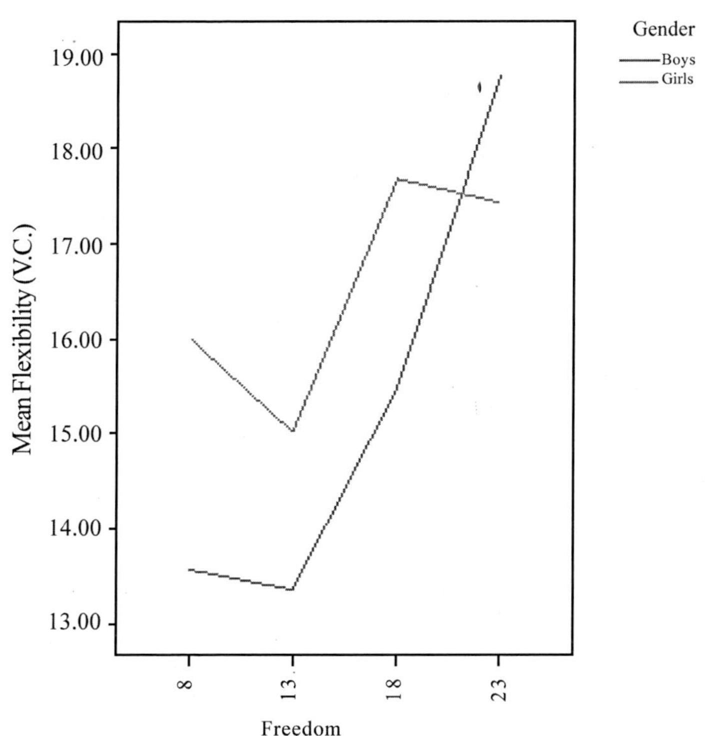

Fig. 4.5.2.2: Graphical Representation of Mean Flexibility Scores in Non-Verbal Creativity Test with Freedom for Boys and Girls on the Same Axes

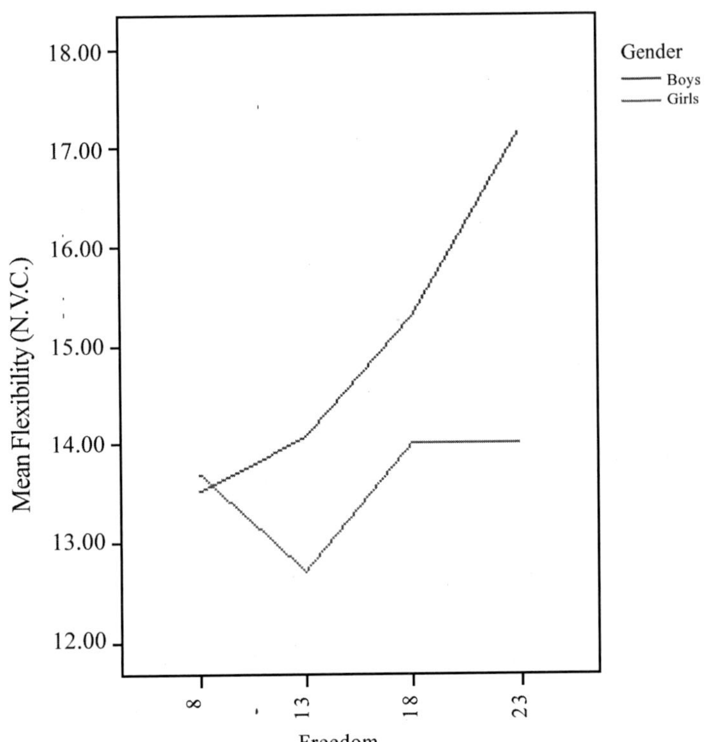

Visual comparison had been drawn in Figure 4.5.2.1 and Figure 4.5.2.2 between Boys and Girls on the Mean Flexibility - Freedom graphs. Obviously, for both verbal and non-verbal creativity, Flexibility increased with the increase of Freedom. Girls' Flexibility (Verbal Creativity) scores were greater than the boys in Figure 4.5.2.1. But Boys' Flexibility (Non-verbal Creativity) scores were greater than the girls' in Figure 4.5.2.2.

Table 4.5.3: Mean Scores of Originality and Class Intervals of Freedom

Freedom Class Interval	*Mid-point of Class Interval*	*Mean Verbal Fluency*		*Mean Non-verbal Fluency*	
		Boys	*Girls*	*Boys*	*Girls*
6 - 10	8	28.33	33.78	26.09	26.50
11 - 15	13	28.00	30.09	25.68	24.23
16 - 20	18	32.81	35.62	26.70	28.48
21 - 25	23	39.67	40.17	30.39	29.78

Fig. 4.5.3.1: Graphical Representation of Mean Originality Scores in Verbal Creativity Test with Freedom for Boys and Girls on the Same Axes

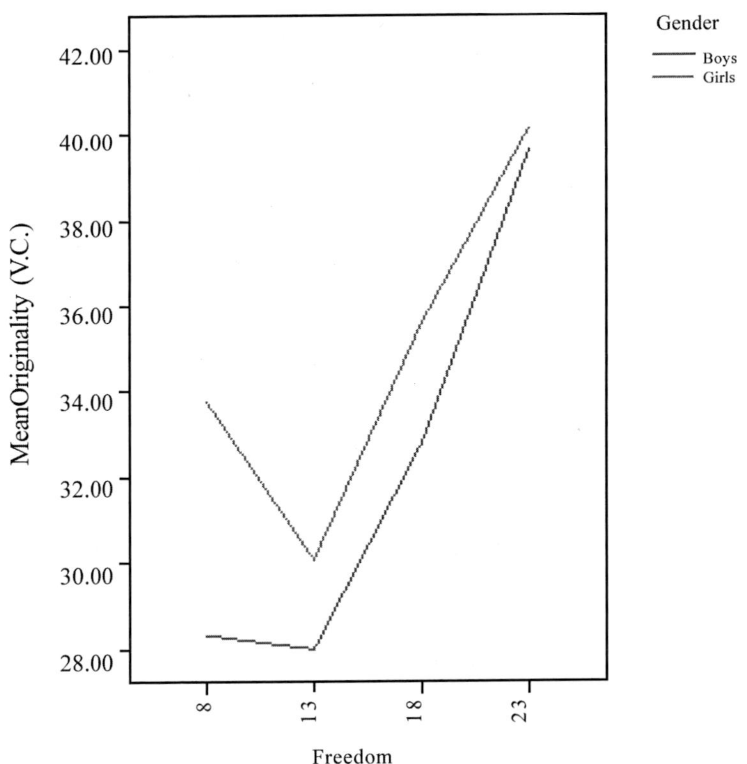

Fig. 4.5.3.2: Graphical Representation of Mean Originality Scores in Non-Verbal Creativity Test with Freedom for Boys and Girls on the Same Axes

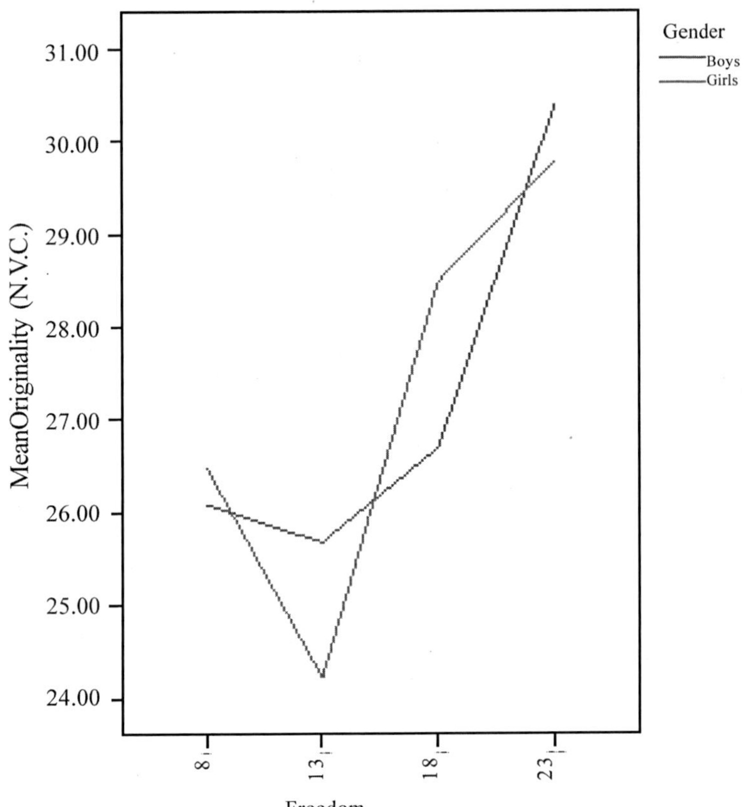

In the Figure 4.5.3.1 and Figured 4.5.3.2, the Multi-line graphs showed that Originality (both verbal and non-verbal) gradually increased with the increase of Freedom. Girls' graph lain on the boys' graph in the Figure 4.5.3.1 which indicated that girls' scores were greater than the boys' scores. In the Figure 4.5.3.2, girls' scores were low at the middle point of Freedom. After that, both graphs gradually increased with the increase of Freedom.

Table 4.5.4: Mean Scores of Fluency and Class Intervals of Socio-economic Status

Socio-economic status Class Interval	*Mid-point of Class Interval*	*Mean Verbal Fluency*		*Mean Non-verbal Fluency*	
		Boys	*Girls*	*Boys*	*Girls*
1 - 20	10.5	34	30.25	27	26.00
21 - 40	30.5	32	28.24	26.92	25.36
41 - 60	50.5	30.31	32.00	26.93	26.50
61 - 80	70.5	30.67	32.44	26.62	24.19
81 - 100	90.5	29.17	33.00	25.41	26.38
101 - 120	110.5	30.74	32.21	28.16	27.59
121 - 140	130.5	36.67	33.78	35.17	26.00
141 - 160	150.5	41.50	33.50	36.00	25.67
161 - 180	170.5	29.67	45.00	28.00	27.50
181 - 200	190.5	43.00	37.00	36.00	26.00

Fig. 4.5.4.1: Graphical Representation of Mean Fluency Scores in Verbal Creativity Test with Socio-economic Status for Boys and Girls on the Same Axes

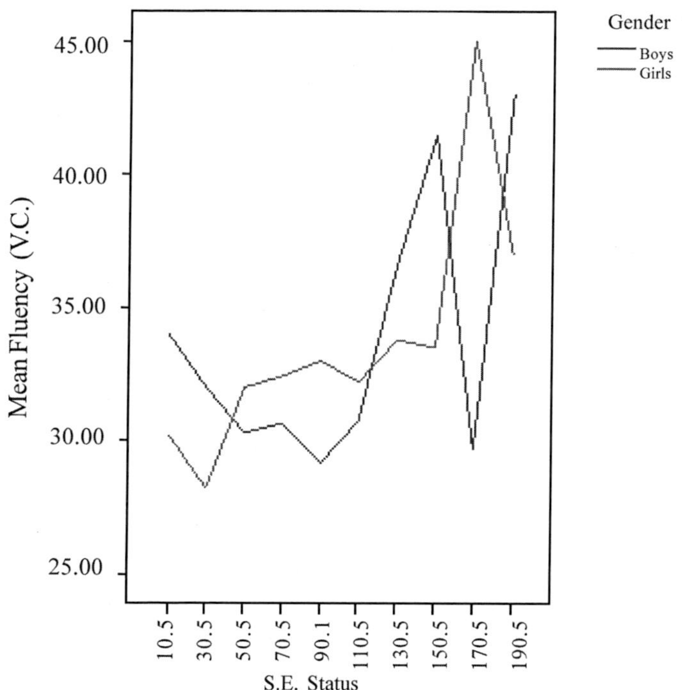

Fig. 4.5.4.2: Graphical Representation of Mean Fluency Scores in Non-Verbal Creativity Test with Socio-economic Status for Boys and Girls on the Same Axes

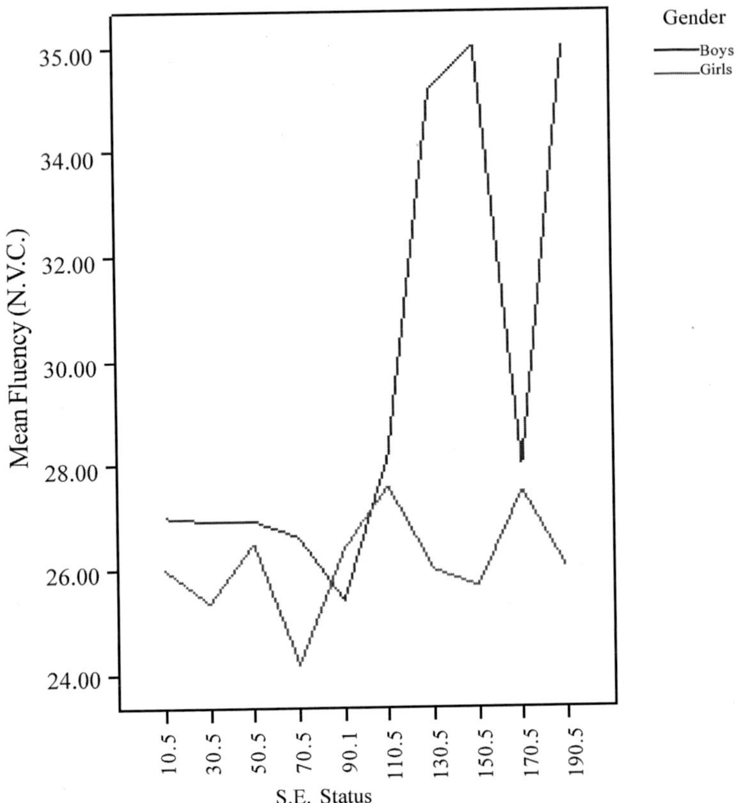

In the Figure 4.5.4.1 and Figure 4.5.4.2 the Multi-line graphs were mostly haphazard. Though the graphs increased upwards with the increase of Socio-economic Status, that was not uniform for both Boys and Girls. The Boys' graphs suddenly fell down at high scores of Socio-economic Status. It indicated that Fluency scores were very low for a few of high Socio-economic scores. In the Figure 4.5.4.2, the Girls' scores were lower than the Boys'.

Table 4.5.5: Mean Scores of Flexibility and Class Intervals of Socio-economic Status

Socio-economic status Class Interval	*Mid-point of Class Interval*	*Mean Verbal Fluency*		*Mean Non-verbal Fluency*	
		Boys	*Girls*	*Boys*	*Girls*
1 - 20	10.5	18	15	17	11.25
21 - 40	30.5	15.84	12.16	14.30	12.00
41 - 60	50.5	14.67	16.46	14.19	13.46
61 - 80	70.5	14.93	15.81	15.35	12.41
81 - 100	90.5	13.30	17.36	13.52	13.50
101 - 120	110.5	14.57	17.21	16.05	15.17
121 - 140	130.5	19.50	18.39	18.50	14.83
141 - 160	150.5	23.00	16.00	23.00	12.17
161 - 180	170.5	12.33	25.50	13.00	13.00
181 - 200	190.5	21.00	22.50	29.00	13.50

Fig. 4.5.5.1: Graphical Representation of Mean Flexibility Scores in Verbal Creativity Test with Socio-economic Status for Boys and Girls on the Same Axes

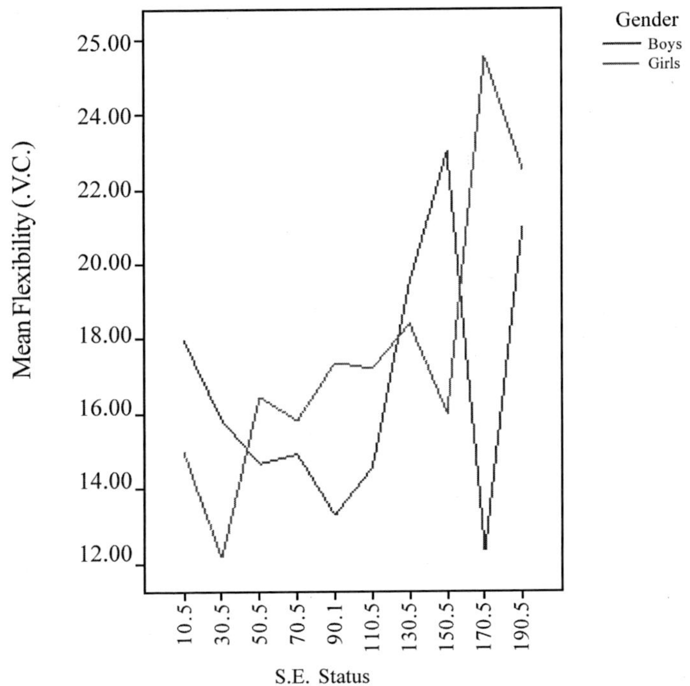

Fig. 4.5.5.2: Graphical Representation of Mean Flexibility Scores in Non-Verbal Creativity Test with Socio-economic Status for Boys and Girls on the Same Axes

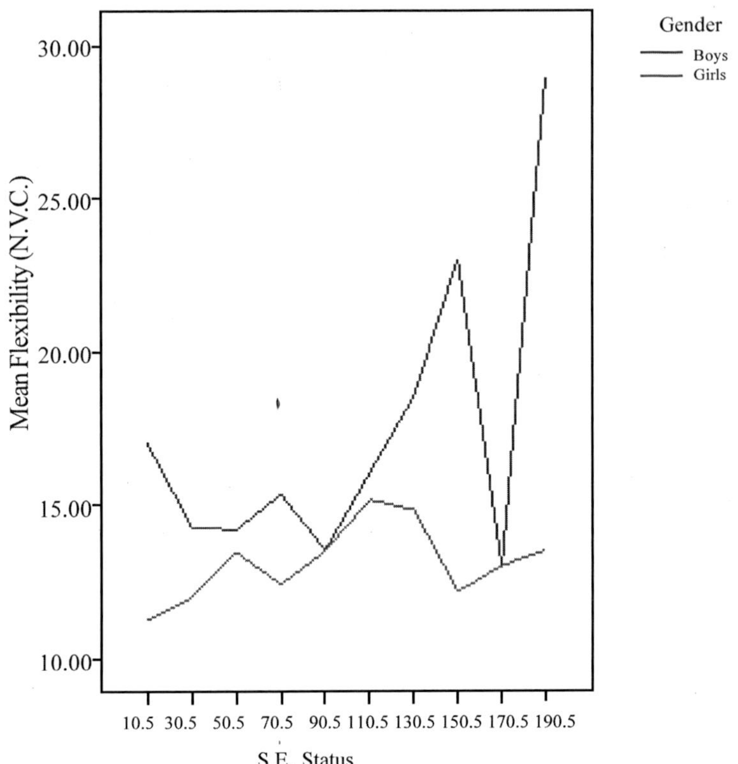

In the Figure 4.5.5.1 and Figure 4.5.5.2, the Multi-line graphs were also haphazardly increased with the increase of Socio-economic Status for both Boys and Girls. Boys' graphs in both cases suddenly fell down at a certain mid-point of class interval of Socio-economic Status. It was found from the Figure 4.5.5.2 that the girls' scores were lower than the boys'.

Table 4.5.6: Mean Scores of Originality and Class Intervals of Socio-economic Status

Socio-economic status Class Interval	*Mid-point of Class Interval*	*Mean Verbal Fluency*		*Mean Non-verbal Fluency*	
		Boys	*Girls*	*Boys*	*Girls*
1 - 20	10.5	37	26.50	44	21.25
21 - 40	30.5	33.88	26.56	23	23.96
41 - 60	50.5	30.26	33.43	26.70	25.03
61 - 80	70.5	30.16	33.25	25.02	25.09
81 - 100	90.5	29.17	33.21	26.06	25.93
101 - 120	110.5	32.52	34.88	28.94	30.44
121 - 140	130.5	41.16	39.22	34.67	30.28
141 - 160	150.5	49.00	38.00	45.50	27.83
161 - 180	170.5	26.67	65.50	31.33	28.50
181 - 200	190.5	49.00	45.00	52.00	37.00

Fig. 4.5.6.1: Graphical Representation of Mean Originality Scores in Verbal Creativity Test with Socio-economic Status for Boys and Girls on the Same Axes

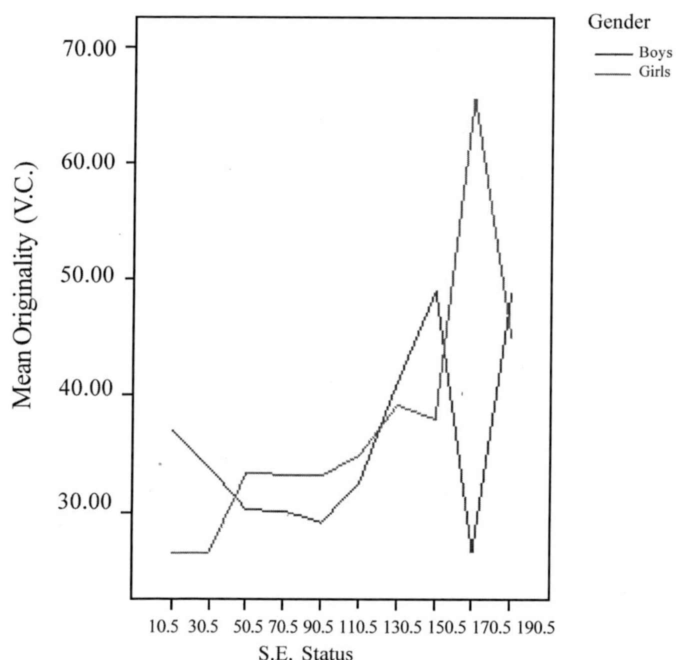

Fig. 4.5.6.2: Graphical Representation of Mean Originality Scores in Non-Verbal Creativity Test with Socio-economic Status for Boys and Girls on the Same Axes

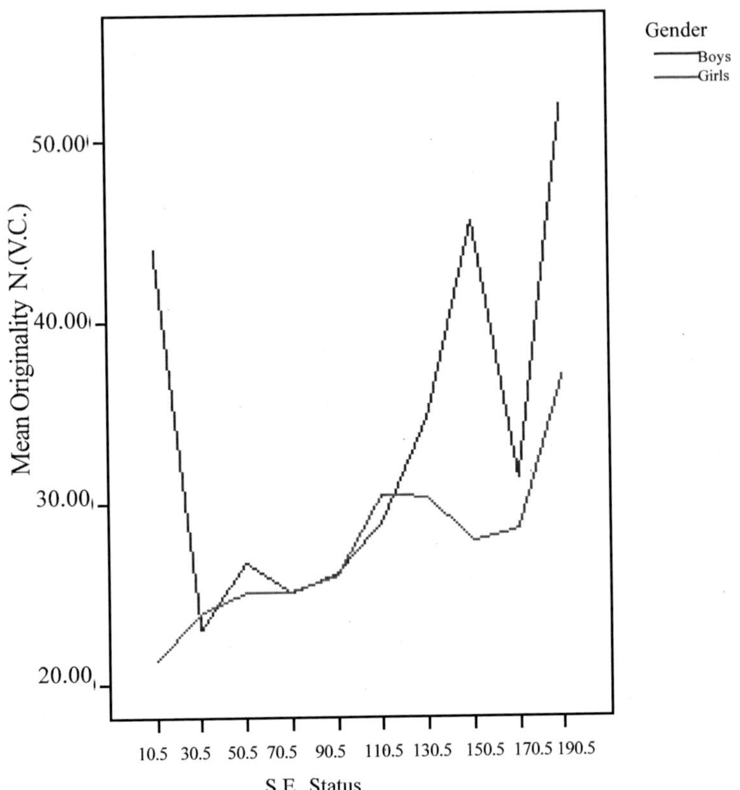

The relationships between Originality and Socio-economic status for both verbal and non-verbal creativity were shown in the Figure 4.5.6.1 and Figure 4.5.6.2 for Boys and Girls on the same axes. Though the Multi-line graphs haphazardly increased with the increase of Socio-economic Status, the Boys' graphs fell down at a certain high Socio-economic Status score. The Girls' graphs were more or less uniform than the Boys'.

PART - IV

INFERENTIAL STATISTICS

Part-IV dealt with the analysis and interpretation by means of Inferential Statistics, i.e. One-way ANOVA and t-test. When the F-values were significant, t-tests had been employed to know the groups in details.

To test the significance of an obtained difference, one must first have the standard error of the difference of the two means as it is reasonable to expect that the difference between two means will be subject to sampling error. From the difference between the sample means and its standard error one can determine whether a difference probably exist between the population.

4.6 Determination of the Significance of Difference in Mean Scores

For inferential statistics, the sample was divided into two groups in accordance with gender - Boys and Girls. The whole analysis was done with respect to this stratum. Data of both Boys and Girls groups were arranged according to their ascending order of scores in each of independent variables viz.; Freedom of students, Socio-economic Status, separately. After that each group again was divided into three sub-groups viz., High, Middle and Low on the basis of 27% statistical rule. For that, out of the whole sample of 372 students of Class VIII and Class IX, number of students existed in each sub-group with the gender differences was as follows:

The above frequency distributions in the sub-groups were also represented in the figure 4.3.2 and figure 4.3.3 respectively.

Variance is a mathematical way of describing the variability between scores in a distribution. The Theory of Analysis of Variance is based on a single fact; in case of two estimates of the variance of a single population, they should be approximately equal.

The value of analysis of variance (ANOVA) in testing hypothesis is strikingly demonstrated in the problems in which the significance of differences among several means are desired. F-tests were adopted by the present researcher on selected groups to know

Table – 4.6.1: Sub-groups of the Whole Sample for Inferential Statistics

GroupItem	*Boys' Group*				*Girls' Group*				*Total(Boys + Girls)*
	High	*Middle*	*Low*	*Total*	*High*	*Middle*	*Low*	*Total*	
Frequency	49	81	49	179	52	89	52	193	372
Percent	27.4%	45.3%	27.4%	100%	26.9%	46.1%	26.9%	100%	100%

whether there were differences between the genders and between the strata (High and Low).

Reasons for adopting the F-tests in the present study:

a) The condition of independent observation was satisfied.

b) The condition of population distribution was assumed to be normal in the present study.

c) By selecting the same number of the students in each group (High or Low), the homogeneity condition was also satisfied.

Since all the conditions were satisfied in the present cases, the F-tests were employed for finding out the significance of differences in mean scores. Since, the F-value was not found significant even at the 0.05 level, the researcher did not feel the necessity of employing t-tests for finding out the significance of differences between the two groups.

4.6.1 Creativity in Relation to Gender

Children's creativity may or may not be varied with their gender difference. Some study reveals that there is no significant difference between boys and girls in their creativity. Again, some researches show that boys are more creative than girls.

From Table - 4.1.1 scores of Fluency, Flexibility and Originality components of both verbal and non-verbal creativity in respect of boys and girls were taken into consideration for one-way ANOVA. One-way ANOVA first confirmed that whether the difference of mean scores of Boys and Girls groups was significant or not by the F-value with corresponding their level of significance. If the F-test was significant, then t-test was applied for that particular case.

4.6.1.1 Fluency Component and Gender Difference

H_1: There would be no significant difference between boys and girls in Fluency scores of verbal and non-verbal creativity.

To find out the significance of the difference between mean scores of Fluency component of both verbal creativity and non-verbal creativity as obtained by boys and girls, one-way ANOVA had been done, as shown in the Table 4.6.2

Table - 4.6.2: Summary of One-Way ANOVA for Gender Difference with Dependent Variables (Fluency, Flexibility, Originality)

Components		*Sum of Squares*	*df*	*Mean Square*	*F*	*Sig.*
Fu_V.C	Between Groups	209.272	1	209.272	2.890	0.090
	Within Groups	26790.685	370	72.407		
	Total	26999.957	371			
Fx_V.C	Between Groups	216.328	1	216.328	4.728	0.030
	Within Groups	16930.605	370	45.758		
	Total	17146.933	371			
Or_V.C	Between Groups	477.910	1	477.910	3.340	0.068
	Within Groups	52943.885	370	143.092		
	Total	53421.796	371			
Fu_N.V.C	Between Groups	105.594	1	105.594	2.195	0.139
	Within Groups	17799.299	370	48.106		
	Total	17904.892	371			
Fx_N.V.C	Between Groups	188.822	1	188.822	7.594	0.006
	Within Groups	9199.723	370	24.864		
	Total	9388.546	371			
Or_N.V.C	Between Groups	.238	1	0.238	0.002	0.962
	Within Groups	39019.964	370	105.459		
	Total	39020.202	371			

Observation

It was seen from the above Table 4.6.2 that the obtained F-value of Fluency component of verbal creativity (Fu_V.C) was 2.890 and level of significance was 0.090, and the F-value of that component for non-verbal creativity (Fu_N.V.C.) was 2.195 and level of significance was 0.139.

Interpretation

In case of Fluency component of verbal creativity the F-value ($F = 2.890$, $df = 1$ & 370, $P > 0.05$) was not significant at the 0.05 level of significance.

Again, for the Fluency component of non-verbal creativity, the F-value ($F = 2.195$, $df = 1$ & 370, $p > 0.05$) also was not significant at the 0.05 level of significance. Thus, the null hypothesis H1 was accepted. That meant, there was no significant difference between boys and girls in Fluency scores of both verbal and non-verbal creativity.

4.6.1.2 Flexibility Components and Gender Differences

H_2 : There would be no significant difference between boys and girls in Flexibility scores of verbal and non-verbal creativity.

One-way ANOVA as shown in the Table 4.6.2 had determined the significance of the difference between mean scores of Flexibility component as obtained by boys and girls by the F-test.

Observation

It was observed from the Table 4.6.2 that the F-value of Flexibility component of Verbal Creativity (Fx_V.C) was 4.728 at the level of significance. 0.030. Again, the F-value of Flexibility component of non-verbal creativity (Fx_N.V.C) was 7.594 and the level of significance was 0.006.

Interpretation

The F-value of Flexibility component of verbal creativity was 4.728 ($F = 4.728$, $df = 1$ & 370, $p < 0.05$) which was significant at the level of significance 0.05.

In case of non-verbal creativity, the F-value of Flexibility component was 7.594 ($F = 7.594$, $df = 1$ & 370, $p < 0.01$) which was highly significant at the 0.01 level of significance.

As the F-values were significant for both verbal and non-verbal creativity between the mean scores of Flexibility component as obtained by the boys and girls, t-tests had been done for both cases to know the groups in details.

Observation

It was found from the Table 4.6.3 that the mean scores of Flexibility of Verbal Creativity of Boys and Girls groups were 14.89 and 16.41 respectively. Here the obtained 't'-value was 2.174 and 0.030 was level of significance.

Interpretation

In the Table 4.6.3, the mean score of Flexibility of Verbal Creativity of Girls group was 16.41 which was greater than that of

Table - 4.6.3: Showing Significance of the Difference Between Means of Flexibility V. C.) for Boys and Girls Groups

Component	*Gender*	*N*	*Mean*	*SD*	*SEm*	*MD*	*SED*	*t*	*df*	*Sig. (2-tailed)*
Fx_V.C	Girls	193	16.41	6.913	0.498	1.526	0.702	2.174	370	0.030
	Boys	179	14.89	6.601	0.493					

Boys group (14.89). Also, the 't' value was 2.174 (t = 2.174, df = 370, p < 0.05) which was significant at 0.05 level of significance. So, the Girls group was superior to the Boys Group in respect to Flexibility of Verbal Creativity.

Observation

The above Table 4.6.4 showed that the means scores of Flexibility of Non-verbal creativity of Boys and Girls were 14.87 and 13.45 respectively. Here the 't' value was -2.756 and the level of significance was 0.006.

Interpretation

In the Table 4.6.4, the 't'-value was -2.756 (t = -2.756, df = 370, p < 0.01) which was also significant at 0.01 level of significance. The negative sign indicated that the mean score of Girls group (13.45) was less than that of Boys group (14.87). So, the difference between the mean scores of Boys and Girls groups was significant but Boys group was superior to the Girls group in respect to Flexibility of Non-verbal Creativity.

From the above discussion it might be interpreted that the hypothesis H2 was not accepted. In other words, significant difference existed between Boys and Girls group in Flexibility mean scores of verbal and non-verbal creativity. But, in Flexibility of Verbal Creativity Girls were superior to Boys and in Flexibility component of non-verbal creativity Boys were advanced to Girls.

4.6.1.3 Originality Component and Gender Difference

H_3: There would be no significant difference between boys and girls in Originality scores of verbal and non-verbal creativity.

In the Table 4.6.2, one-way ANOVA had determined the significance of the difference between mean scores of Originality component as obtained by boys and girls by the F-test.

Observation

The Table 4.6.2 showed that the F-value of Originality component of verbal creativity (Or_V.C) was 3.340 at the level of significance

Table - 4.6.4: Showing Significance of the Difference Between Means of Flexibility (N. V. C.) for Boys and Girls Groups

Component	*Gender*	*N*	*Mean*	*SD*	*SEm*	*MD*	*SED*	*t*	*df*	*Sig. (2-tailed)*
Fx_N.V.C	Girls	193	13.45	4.731	0.341	-1.426	0.517	-2.756	370	0.006
	Boys	179	14.87	5.248	0.392					

0.068. Again, the F-value of Originality component of non-verbal creativity (Or_N. V. C) was 0.002 and the level of significance was 0.962.

Interpretation

In case of Originality component of verbal creativity the F-value ($F = 3.340$, $df = 1$ & 370, $p > 0.05$) was not significant at 0.05 level of significance.

Again, for the Originality component of non-verbal creativity, the F-value ($F = 0.002$, $df = 1$ & 370, $p > 0.05$) was also insignificant at the 0.05 level of significance.

Thus, the null hypothesis H3 was accepted. That meant, there was no significant difference between boys and girls in Originality scores of both verbal and non-verbal creativity.

4.6.2 Creativity and Freedom

Freedom of thought and actions enjoyed by the students in the family may be favourable to foster creativity in him or her. Freedom of thought gives the students to make original ideas in practices and to become more fluent and flexible in different actions.

4.6.2.1 Creativity with Freedom and Restriction Group Boys

Data of 179 students of Boys group were separated from the original sheets (Table 4.1.1) and were arranged in descending order with respect to their obtained Freedom scores. Then the upper 49 boys were of High group called 'Freedom group' and the lower 49 boys were of Low group called 'Restriction group' on the basis of 27% statistical rule.

Fluency, Flexibility and Originality scores obtained by 'Freedom group' boys and 'Restriction group' boys were taken into consideration for one-way ANOVA. One-way ANOVA first confirmed that whether the difference of means scores between 'Freedom group' boys and 'Restriction group' boys was significant or not by the F-value with corresponding their level of significance.

If the F-test was significant, the t-test was applied for that particular case.

Table - 4.6.5: Summary of One-Way ANOVA for Freedom of High & Low (Freedom and Restriction) Groups Boys with Dependent Variables (Fluency, Flexibility, Originality)

Components of Creativity		*Sum of Squares*	*df*	*Mean Square*	*F*	*Sig.*
Fu_V.C	Between Groups	955.469	1	955.469	15.346	0.000
	Within Groups	5977.061	96	62.261		
	Total	6932.531	97			
Fu_N.V.C	Between Groups	480.500	1	480.500	9.588	0.003
	Within Groups	4810.816	96	50.113		
	Total	5291.316	97			
Fx_V.C	Between Groups	388.010	1	388.010	12.013	0.001
	Within Groups	3100.735	96	32.299		
	Total	3488.745	97			
Fx_N.V.C	Between Groups	183.224	1	183.224	7.128	0.009
	Within Groups	2467.755	96	25.706		
	Total	2650.980	97			
Or_V.C	Between Groups	2282.949	1	2282.949	23.461	0.000
	Within Groups	9341.551	96	97.308		
	Total	11624.500	97			
Or_N.V.C	Between Groups	800.000	1	800.000	7.666	0.007
	Within Groups	10018.204	96	104.356		
	Total	10818.204	97			

H_4: There would be significant difference between Freedom and Restriction groups boys in Fluency, Flexibility and Originality scores of verbal and non-verbal creativity.

4.6.2.1.1 Fluency Component and 'Freedom' and 'Restriction' Groups Boys

To find out that the significance of the difference between mean scores of Fluency component of both verbal creativity and non-verbal creativity as obtained by the Freedom group boys and Restriction group boys, one-way ANOVA had been done as shown in the Table - 4.6.5.

Observation

It was seen from the Table 4.6.5 that the obtained F-value of Fluency component of Verbal Creativity (Fu_V.C) was 15.346 and level of significance was 0.000, and the F-value of that component of non-verbal creativity (Fu_N.V.C) was 9.588 and level of significance was 0.003.

Interpretation

In verbal creativity, the Fluency component contained the F-value 15.346 ($F = 15.346$, $df = 1$ and 96, $p < 0.01$) for 'Freedom' and 'Restriction' groups boys. This F-value was highly significant at 0.01 level of significance.

In non-verbal creativity, the F-value of Fluency component for the two groups 'Freedom' and 'Restriction' was 9.588 which was also significant at 0.01 level of significance.

Thus, it might be implied that for both verbal and non-verbal creativity, there was a significant difference between the 'Freedom group' and 'Restriction group' boys in Fluency. But which group was more advanced to another and how much it was, to know the details 't'-test had been applied in both cases.

Observation

It was found from the Table 4.6.6 that the mean scores of Fluency of Verbal Creativity of 'Freedom' and 'Restriction' groups were 35.24 and 29.00 respectively. Here the 't' value was 3.917 and the level of significance was 0.000.

Interpretation

In the Table 4.6.6, the mean score of Fluency (V. C.) of Freedom group was 35.24 which was greater than that of Restriction group (29.00). The 't' value ($t = 3.917$, $df = 96$, $p < 0.01$) was significant

Table - 4.6.6: Showing Significance of the Difference Between Means of Fluency (V. C) for Freedom and Restriction Groups Boys

Component	*Group*	*N*	*Mean*	*SD*	*SEm*	*MD*	*SED*	*t*	*df*	*Sig. (2-tailed)*
Fu_V.C	Freedom	49	35.24	7.284	1.041	6.245	1.594	3.917	96	0.000
	Restriction	49	29.00	8.453	1.208					

Table - 4.6.7: Showing Significance of the Difference Between Means of Fluency (N.V.C) for Freedom and Restriction Groups Boys

Component	*Group*	*N*	*Mean*	*SD*	*SEm*	*MD*	*SED*	*t*	*df*	*Sig. (2-tailed)*
Fu_N.V.C	Freedom	49	29.41	7.494	1.071	4.429	1.43	3.097	96	0.003
	Restriction	49	24.98	6.638	0.948					

at 0.01 level of significance. So, the 'Freedom group' was superior to 'Restriction group' for boys in respect to their scores of Fluency of Verbal Creativity.

Observation

It was seen from the Table - 4.6.7 that the means scores of Fluency of Non-verbal Creativity of 'Freedom' and 'Restriction' groups were 29.41 and 24.98 respectively. The obtained 't' value was 3.097 and the level of significance was 0.003.

Interpretation

As the mean score of Fluency component of non-verbal creativity (Fu_N.V.C) of 'Freedom group' was greater than that of 'Restriction group' and the 't'-value ($t = 3.097$, $df = 96$, $p < 0.01$) was significant at 0.01 level of significance, the 'Freedom group' was also advanced to 'Restriction group' for boys.

From the above discussions, it might be interpreted that there was a significant difference between 'Freedom group' and 'Restriction group' of boys and 'Freedom group' was always superior to the 'Restriction group' in Fluency of both verbal and non-verbal creativity.

4.6.2.1.2 Flexibility Component and 'Freedom' and 'Restriction' Groups Boys

One-way ANOVA had been done as shown in the Table 4.6.5 to determine the significance of the difference between mean scores of Flexibility component of both verbal and non-verbal creativity as obtained by the Freedom group and Restriction group boys.

Observation

It was found from the Table 4.6.5 that the obtained F-value of Flexibility component of verbal creativity (Fx_V.C) was 12.013 and the level of significance was 0.001, and the F-value of that component of non-verbal creativity (Fx_N. V.C) was 7.128 and the level of significance was 0.009.

sTable - 4.6.8: Showing Significance of the Difference Between Means of Flexibility (V. C) for 'Freedom' & 'Restriction' Group Boys

Component	*Group*	*N*	*Mean*	*SD*	*SEm*	*MD*	*SED*	*t*	*df*	*Sig. (2-tailed)*
Fx_V.C	Freedom	49	17.94	5.080	0.726	3.980	1.148	3.466	96	0.001
	Restriction	49	13.96	6.228	0.890					

Table-4.6.9: Showing Significance of the Difference Between Means of Flexibility (N.V.C) for 'Freedom' and 'Restriction' Group Boys

Component	Group	N	Mean	SD	SEm	MD	SED	t	df	Sig. (2-tailed)
Fx_N.V.C	Freedom	49	16.47	5.176	0.739	2.735	1.024	2.670	96	0.009
	Restriction	49	13.73	4.961	0.709					

Interpretation

The F-value of Flexibility component of Verbal Creativity (Fx_V.C) was (F = 12.013, df = 1 and 96, p = 0.001) highly significant at 0.01 level of significance.

Again, the F-value of Flexibility component of non-verbal creativity (Fx_N.V.C) was (F=7.128, df = 1 and 96, p = 0.009) also significant at 0.01 level of significance.

It implied that for both verbal and non-verbal creativity, there was a significant difference between the 'Freedom group' and 'Restriction group' boys in Flexibility. But which group was more advanced to another and how much it was, to know the details 't'-test had been applied in both cases.

Observation

From the Table 4.6.8, it was found that the mean scores of Flexibility of Verbal Creativity of 'Freedom' and 'Restriction' groups were 17.94 and 13.96 respectively. Here the t-value was 3.466 and significance level was 0.001.

Interpretation

In the above Table 4.6.8, the mean score of Flexibility (V.C) of Freedom group was 17.94 which was greater than that of Restriction group (13.96) . The 't'-value (t = 3.466, df = 96, p < 0.01) was significant at 0.01 level of significance. Hence, the 'Freedom group' was superior to the 'Restriction group' for boys in respect to their scores of Flexibility of Verbal Creativity.

Observation

From the Table 4.6.9, it was seen that the mean scores of Flexibility of non-verbal creativity of 'Freedom' and 'Restriction' groups were 16.47 and 13.73 respectively. The obtained 't'-value was 2.670 and significance level was 0.009.

Interpretation

In that observation, the mean score of Flexibility (N. V. C.) of Freedom group was 16.47 which was higher than that of Restriction group (13.73). Here, the 't'-value (t = 2.670, df = 96, p < 0.01) was significant at 0.01 level of significance. Hence the Freedom group was advanced to the Restriction group for boys in mean scores of Flexibility of non-verbal creativity.

So, it implied that for both verbal and non-verbal creativity, there was a significant difference between the 'Freedom group' and 'Restriction group' boys in Flexibility and 'Freedom group' was always superior to the 'Restriction group' in Flexibility of both verbal and non-verbal creativity.

4.6.2.1.3 Originality Component and 'Freedom' and Restriction Groups Boys

To determine the significance of the difference between mean scores of Originality component of both verbal and non-verbal creativity as obtained by the Freedom group and Restriction group boys, One-way ANOVA had been done as shown in the Table 4.6.5.

Observation

The F-value of Originality component of verb al creativity (Or_V.C) was (F = 23.461, df = 1 and 96, p = 0.000) highly significant at 0.01 level of significance.

Again, the F-value of Originality component of non-verbal creativity (Or_N.V.C) was (F = 7.666, df = 1 and 96, p = 0.007) also significant at 0.01 level of significance.

Hence, there was a significant difference between the 'Freedom group' and 'Restriction group' boys in Originality component of both verbal and non-verbal creativity. But which group was more advanced to another and how much it was, to know the details 't'-test had been applied in both cases.

Observation

It was seen from the Table 4.6.10 that the mean scores of Originality of Verbal Creativity of 'Freedom' and 'Restriction' groups were 37.76 and 28.10 respectively. The 't'-value was 4.844 and level of significance was 0.000.

Table - 4.6.10: Showing Significance of the Difference Between Means of Originality (V. C) for 'Freedom' and 'Restriction' Group Boys

Component	*Group*	*N*	*Mean*	*SD*	*SEm*	*MD*	*SED*	*t*	*df*	*Sig. (2-tailed)*
Or_V.C	Freedom 49	37.76	9.514	1.359	9.653	1.993	4.844	96	0.000	
	Restriction	49	28.10	10.203	1.458					

Table-4.6.11: Showing Significance of the Difference Between Means of Originality (N.V.C) for 'Freedom' and 'Restriction' Group Boys

Component	*Group*	*N*	*Mean*	*SD*	*SEm*	*MD*	*SED*	*t*	*df*	*Sig. (2-tailed)*
Or_N.V.C	Freedom 49		30.20	11.740	1.677	5.714	2.064	2.769	96	0.007
	Restriction		49	24.49	8.419	1.203				

Interpretation

Table 4.6.10 revealed that Freedom group was greater than Restriction group in mean score of Originality (V. C.) and mean difference was 9.653. The 't'-value was significant at 0.01 level of significance with df = 96. It suggested that the 'Freedom group' of boys was significantly superior to the 'Restriction group' of Boys in Originality of Verbal Creativity.

Observation

It was to be noted from the Table - 4.6.11 that the mean scores of 'Freedom' and 'Restriction' groups were 30.20 and 24.49 respectively in Originality component of non-verbal creativity. The mean difference between the two groups was 5.714. The Table also showed that the 't'-value was 2.769 at 0.007 level of significance with df = 96.

Interpretation

It was evident from the Table 4.6.11 that the 'Freedom group' was higher than the 'Restriction group' by 5.714 in the mean score of Originality (N.V.C). Here, 't'-value was also significant at 0.01 level of significance ($t = 2.769$, $df = 96$, $p < 0.01$). With regard to the mean scores of 'Freedom' & 'Restriction' in Originality of non-verbal creativity, the 'Freedom group' was significantly greater than the 'Restriction group'.

From the above discussions, it might be interpreted that a significant difference existed between 'Freedom group' and 'Restriction group' of boys and the 'Freedom group' was always advanced to the 'Restriction group' in Originality of both verbal and non-verbal creativity.

From the detail discussions, it might be concluded that the 'Freedom group' of boys was always superior to the 'Restriction group' in mean scores of Fluency, Flexibility as well as in Originality components of both Verbal Creativity and Non-verbal Creativity. That meant, there was a significant difference between 'Freedom group' and 'Restriction group' of boys in Fluency, Flexibility and Originality scores of both verbal and non-verbal creativity. So, the hypothesis H4 was totally accepted.

4.6.2.2 Creativity with Freedom Group and Restriction Group Girls

Data of 193 students of Girls group were separated from the original sheets (Table 4.1.1) and were arranged in descending order with respect to their obtained Freedom scores. Then the upper 52 girls were of High group called 'Freedom group' and the lower 52 girls were of Low group called 'Restriction group' on the basis of 27% statistical rule.

Fluency, Flexibility and Originality scores obtained by 'Freedom group' girls and 'Restriction group' girls were taken into consideration for one-way ANOVA. One-way ANOVA first confirms that whether the difference of mean scores between 'Freedom group' girls and 'Restriction group' girls was significant or not by the F-value with correspondence to their level of significance. If the F-test was significant, the t-test was applied for that particular case.

Table - 4.6.12: Summary of One-way ANOVA for Freedom of High and Low (Freedom & Restriction) Groups Girls with Dependent Variables (Fluency, Flexibility, Originality)

Components of Creativity		*Sum of Squares*	*df*	*Mean Square*	*F*	*Sig.*
Fu_V.C	Between Groups	271.385	1	271.385	4.464	0.037
	Within Groups	6200.577	102	60.790		
	Total	6471.962	103			
Fx_V.C	Between Groups	155.087	1	155.087	3.652	0.059
	Within Groups	4332.135	102	42.472		
	Total	4487.221	103			
Or_V.C	Between Groups	1395.779	1	1395.779	8.605	0.004
	Within Groups	16545.058	102	162.206		
	Total	17940.837	103			
Fu_N.V.C	Between Groups	165.010	1	165.010	3.811	0.054
	Within Groups	4416.750	102	43.301		
	Total	4581.760	103			
Fx_N.V.C	Between Groups	74.462	1	74.462	3.375	0.069
	Within Groups	2250.423	102	22.063		
	Total	2324.885	103			
Or_N.V.C	Between Groups	170.087	1	170.087	1.595	0.209
	Within Groups	10873.904	102	106.607		
	Total	11043.990	103			

4.6.2.2.1 Components of Verbal Creativity and 'Freedom' and 'Restriction' Groups Girls:

H_5: There would be significant difference between Freedom and Restriction group girls in Fluency, Flexibility and Originality scores of Verbal Creativity. To determine the significance of the difference between mean scores as obtained by 'Freedom group' and 'Restriction group' girls in Fluency, Flexibility and Originality components of verbal creativity, one-way ANOVA had been done, as shown in the Table 4.6.12.

Observation

It was to be noted from the Table: 4.6.12 that the obtained F-value of Fluency component (Fu_V.C) was 4.464 and level of significance was 0.037, and that of Flexibility component (Fx-V.C) was 3.652 at 0.59 level of significance and that of Originality component (Or_V.C) was 8.605 at 0.004 level of significance.

Interpretation

It was evident from the Table: 4.6.12 that the F-value of Fluency component ($F = 4.464$, df = 1 and 102, $p < 0.05$) was significant only at 0.05 level of significance and that of Flexibility component ($F = 3.642$, df = 1 and 102, $p > 0.05$) was not significant even at 0.05 level of significance. Again, the F-value of Originality component (Or_V.C) was 8.605 ($F = 8.605$, df = 1 and 102, $p < 0.01$) which was highly significant at 0.01 level of significance.

From the above, the F-values of Fluency component and Originality component of verbal creativity were significant. To know the details of the two groups - 'Freedom' and 'Restriction', 't'-tests had been done in these cases.

Observation

The Table: 4.6.13 showed that the mean scores of Fluency of Verbal Creativity of 'Freedom' and 'Restriction' group girls were 34.13 and 30.90 respectively, and the t-value was 2.113 at 0.037 level of significance with df = 102.

Table - 4.6.13: Showing Significance of the Difference Between Means of Fluency (V.C) for Freedom & Restriction Group Girls

Component	*Group*	*N*	*Mean*	*SD*	*SEm*	*MD*	*SED*	*t*	*df*	*Sig. (2-tailed)*
Fu_V.C	Freedom 52	34.13	7.667	1.063	3.231	1.529	2.113	102	0.037	
	Restriction	52	30.90	7.924	1.099					

Table-4.6.14: Showing Significance of the Difference Between Means of Originality (V.C) for 'Freedom' and 'Restriction' Group Girls

Component	*Group*	*N*	*Mean*	*SD*	*SEm*	*MD*	*SED*	*t*	*df*	*Sig. (2-tailed)*
Or_V.C	Freedom 52	38.06	13.172	1.827	7.327	2.498	2.933	102	0.004	
	Restriction	52	30.73	12.284	1.704					

Interpretation

It was evident from the Table 4.6.13 above that the obtained 't'-value ($t = 2.113$, $df = 102$, $p < 0.05$) was significant at only 0.05 level of significance. The 'Freedom group' was advanced to the 'Restriction group' for girls in Fluency of Verbal Creativity.

Observation

In the above Table 4.6.14, the mean scores of Originality component of Verbal Creativity (Or_V.C) of 'Freedom group' and 'Restriction group' were 38.06 and 30.73 respectively and mean difference between them was 7.327. The obtained 't'-value was 2.933 at 0.004 level of significance.

Interpretation

The above Table 4.6.14 revealed that the 'Freedom group' contained the greater mean score (38.06) than that of the 'Restriction group' (30.73). The mean difference between them was also significant as the obtained 't'-value (2.933) was significant at 0.01 level of significance with $df = 102$. That meant, the 'Freedom group' was superior to the 'Restriction group' of girls in Originality (V.C.).

It might be concluded that the 'Freedom group' girls was advanced to the 'Restriction group' girls in Fluency as well as in Originality component of verbal creativity and the differences between the two groups in mean scores were significant. But the difference between the mean scores of them in Flexibility (V.C) was not significant. Hence the hypothesis - H5 might be accepted.

4.6.2.2.2 Components of Non-verbal Creativity and 'Freedom' and 'Restriction' Groups Girls

H_6: There would be significant differences between Freedom and Restriction group girls in Fluency, Flexibility and Originality scores of non-verbal creativity.

One-way ANOVA had been formulated, as shown in the Table 4.6.12 to determine the significance of the difference between mean scores as obtained by 'Freedom group' and 'Restriction group' girls in Fluency, Flexibility and Originality components of non-verbal creativity.

Observation

It was seen from the Table - 4.6.12 that the obtained F-values of Fluency (Fu_N.V.C), Flexibility (Fx_N.V.C) and Originality (Or_N.V.C) were 3.811 (at p = 0.054), 3.375 (at p = 0.069) and 1.595 (at p = 0.209) respectively with df = 1 and 102.

Interpretation

It was evident from the Table 4.6.12 that all the F-values of Fluency, Flexibility and Originality of non-verbal creativity were not significant even at 0.05 level of significance with df = 1 and 102, for the two groups 'Freedom' group and 'Restriction' group girls.

Obviously, the difference between 'Freedom' and 'Restriction' group girls was not significant in Fluency, Flexibility and Originality mean scores. In other words, there was no significant difference between 'Freedom' group and 'Restriction' group in Fluency, Flexibility and Originality of non-verbal creativity. So, the hypothesis - H_6 was totally rejected.

4.6.3 Creativity and Socio-economic Status

Socio-economic Status may influence the child to think widely, fluently and divergently. As the children of High Socio-economic Status family get many scopes to do various works or plays, get many goods to know and how to use in different ways, economic condition helps them to gather knowledge from various fields of life. So, Socio-economic Status may have significant effects on creativity of the students.

4.6.3.1 Creativity with High & Low Socio-economic Status Groups Boys

Data of 179 boys were separated from the original sheets (Table 4.1.1) and then were arranged in descending order with respect to their obtained Socio-economic Status scores. Then the upper 49 boys were of High Socio-economic Status group and the lower 49 boys were of Low Socio-economic Status group on the basis of 27% statistical rule.

Generally, Socio-economic Status (SES) should be categorized in three groups, viz.; High, Middle and Low for analysing and interpretation of data. But the researcher found that there was no significant effect of Middle group on analysis and interpretation of data. For that reason, to reduce complicacy, only High and Low group of Socio-economic Status had been considered in this study.

One-way ANOVA design had been formulated on the basis of Fluency, Flexibility and Originality scores as obtained by the boys of High group and Low group of Socio-economic Status. One-way ANOVA confirmed that whether the difference of mean scores between High group SES and Low group SES was significant or not by the F-ratio with level of significance.

Table - 4.6.15: Summary of One-way ANOVA for Socio-economic Status of High and Low Groups Boys with Dependent Variables (Fluency, Flexibility, Originality)

Components of Creativity		*Sum of Squares*	*df*	*Mean Square*	*F*	*Sig.*
Fu_V.C	Between Groups	4.500	1	4.500	0.059	0.809
	Within Groups	7378.694	96	76.861		
	Total	7383.194	97			
Fu_N.V.C	Between Groups	156.898	1	156.898	3.036	0.085
	Within Groups	4960.939	96	51.676		
	Total	5117.837	97			
Fx_V.C	Between Groups	8.582	1	8.582	0.199	0.657
	Within Groups	4146.449	96	43.192		
	Total	4155.031	97			
Fx_N.V.C	Between Groups	110.367	1	110.367	3.903	.051
	Within Groups	2714.980	96	28.281		
	Total	2825.347	97			
Or_V.C	Between Groups	23.510	1	23.510	0.188	0.666
	Within Groups	12029.551	96	125.308		
	Total	12053.061	97			
Or_N.V.C	Between Groups	1242.867	1	1242.867	11.621	0.001
	Within Groups	10267.633	96	106.955		
	Total	11510.500	97			

H_7: There would be significant difference between High and Low Socio-economic Status groups boys in Fluency, Flexibility and Originality scores of verbal and non-verbal creativity.

4.6.3.1.1 Fluency Component and High & Low Socio-economic Status Group Boys

Observation

It was obtained from the Table - 4.6.15 that the F-value of Fluency of verbal creativity (Fu_V.C) was 0.059 at 0.809 level of significance and that of non-verbal creativity (Fu_N.V.C) was 3.036 at 0.085 level of significance.

Interpretation

For both verbal and non-verbal creativity, the F-values of Fluency were not significant at 0.05 level of significance with df = 1 and 96. That meant, the High group SES did not differ from the Low group SES in Fluency mean scores of both verbal and non-verbal creativity.

4.6.3.1.2 Flexibility Component and High & Low Socio-economic Status Groups Boys

Observation

In the Table 4.6.15 the obtained F-value of Flexibility of verbal creativity (Fx_V.C) was 0.199 at 0.657 level of significance and that of non-verbal creativity (Fx_N.V.C) was 3.903 at level of significance 0.051.

Interpretation

Here also the obtained F-values of Flexibility scores of both verbal and non-verbal creativity were not significant even at 0.05 level of significance with df = 1 and 96. Hence, there was no significant difference between High group and Low group SES boys in Flexibility mean scores of both verbal and non-verbal creativity.

4.6.3.1.3 Originality Component and High & Low Socio-economic Status Groups Boys

Observation

It revealed from the Table 4.6.15 that the F-value of Originality of verbal creativity (Or_V.C) was 0.188 and level of significance was 0.666. Again, the F-value of Originality of non-verbal creativity (Or_N.V.C) was 11.621 at 0.001 level of significance.

Interpretation

It was evident from the Table 4.6.15 the F-value of Originality (V. C.) was not significant at 0.05 level of significance. But the F-value of Originality (N. V. C.) was highly significant at 0.01 level of significance. To know the significant difference in detail between the two groups - High and Low SES in Originality of non-verbal creativity, further 't'-test had been applied.

Observation

It was seen from the Table - 4.6.16 that the mean scores of Originality (N.V.C) as obtained by High group SES and Low group SES were 31.20 and 24.08 respectively and mean difference was 7.122. The obtained 't'-value was 3.409 at 0.001 level of significance with df = 96.

Interpretation

It was evident from the Table - 4.6.16 the 't'-value ($t = 3.409$, $df = 96$, $p < 0.01$) was significant at 0.01 level of significance. Again, the High group SES was greater than the Low group SES in mean score of Originality (N.V.C). So, the High group SES was advanced to the Low group SES in Originality of Non-verbal Creativity.

From the earlier discussions as mentioned in the sections 4.6.3.1.1; 4.6.3.1.2 and 4.6.3.1.3, it might be concluded that there was no significant difference between High group SES boys and Low group SES boys in Fluency (both verbal and non-verbal), in Flexibility (both verbal & non-verbal), and in Originality (verbal). In other words, a significant difference existed between the two groups - High & Low SES only in Originality of non-verbal creativity. So, the hypothesis - H_7 might be rejected.

4.6.3.2 Creativity with High & Low Socio-economic Status Groups Girls

Data of 193 girls were arranged in descending order with respect to their obtained Socio-economic Status scores. Then the upper 52 girls were of High Socio-economic Status group and the lower 52 girls were of Low Socio-economic Status group on the basis of 27% statistical rule.

Table-4.6.16: Showing Significance of the Difference Between Means of Originality (N.V.C) for High & Low Socio-economic Status Group Boys

Component	*Group*	*N*	*Mean*	*SD*	*SEm*	*MD*	*SED*	*t*	*df*	*Sig. (2-tailed)*
Or_N.V.C	High	49	31.20	11.195	1.599	7.122	2.089	3.409	96	0.001
	Low	49	24.08	9.412	1.345					

One-way ANOVA design had been adopted to determine the significance of the difference in mean scores of Fluency, Flexibility, Originality of both verbal and non-verbal creativity between High group and Low group Socio-economic Status girls. If the F-test was significant then 't'-test had been applied in that particular case.

Table - 4.6.17: Summary of One-way ANOVA for Socio-economic Status of High & Low Groups Girls with Dependent Variables (Fluency, Flexibility, Originality)

Components of Creativity		*Sum of Squares*	*df*	*Mean Square*	*F*	*Sig.*
Fu_V.C	Between Groups	380.779	1	380.779	4.846	0.030
	Within Groups	8015.058	102	78.579		
	Total	8395.837	103			
Fu_N.V.C	Between Groups	19.471	1	19.471	0.385	0.536
	Within Groups	5162.058	102	50.608		
	Total	5181.529	103			
Fx_V.C	Between Groups	315.010	1	315.010	6.328	0.013
	Within Groups	5077.904	102	49.783		
	Total	5392.913	103			
Fx_N.V.C	Between Groups	106.010	1	106.010	4.889	0.029
	Within Groups	2211.750	102	21.684		
	Total	2317.760	103			
Or_V.C	Between Groups	2106.000	1	2106.000	11.690	0.001
	Within Groups	18375.846	102	180.155		
	Total	20481.846	103			
Or_N.V.C	Between Groups	930.010	1	930.010	7.551	0.007
	Within Groups	12562.904	102	123.166		
	Total	13492.913	103			

H_8: There would be significant difference between High and Low Socio-economic Status groups girls in Fluency, Flexibility and Originality of verbal and non-verbal creativity.

4.6.3.2.1 Fluency Component and High & Low Socio-economic Status Groups Girls

Observation

It was to be noted from the Table - 4.6.17 that the F-value of Fluency (V.C) was 4.846 at 0.030 level of significance and that of

Fluency (N.V.C) was 0.385 at 0.536 level of significance.

Interpretation

The F-value of Fluency of verbal creativity (F = 4.846, df = 1 and 102, p < 0.05) was significant at 0.05 level of significance. That implied, there was a significant difference between High and Low group SES girls in mean score of Fluency (V. C). But the F-value of Fluency of non-verbal creativity (F = 0.385, df = 1 and 102, p > 0.05) was not significant even at 0.05 level of significance.

Observation

The Table - 4.6.18 showed that the mean scores of High group and Low group Socio-economic Status (SES) were 33.81 and 29.98 respectively. Here the obtained 't'-value was 2.201 at 0.030 level of significance.

Interpretation

It was obtained from the Table - 4.6.18 that the 't'-value was significant at 0.05 level of significance and mean score of High group SES was greater than that of Low group SES. So, the High group SES girls was significantly advanced to the Low group SES girls in mean score Fluency (V.C).

From the earlier discussion, it might be implied that the High group SES girls was superior to the Low group SES girls in Fluency of verbal creativity but in Fluency of non-verbal creativity there was no significant difference between High and Low groups SES girls.

4.6.3.2.2 Flexibility Component and High and Low Socio-economic Status Group Girls

Observation

It was seen from the Table 4.6.17 that the F-values of Flexibility scores of both verbal and non-verbal creativity were 6.328 at 0.013 level of significance and 4.889 at 0.029 level of significance respectively.

Table-4.6.18: Showing Significance of the Difference Between Means of Fluency (V. C) for High & Low Groups Socio-economic Status Girls

Component	*Group*	*N*	*Mean*	*SD*	*SEm*	*MD*	*SED*	*t*	*df*	*Sig. (2-tailed)*
Fu_V.C	High	52	33.81	9.350	1.297	3.827	1.738	2.201	102	0.030
	Low	52	29.98	8.351	1.158					

Interpretation

From the Table 4.6.17 it was evident that the F-value of Flexibility of both verbal and non-verbal creativity were significant at 0.05 level of significance with df = 1 and 102. That meant, significant difference existed between the two groups - High and Low SES girls in both types of Flexibility. Further 't'-test had been applied to know the advanced group and mean score difference between them in both cases.

Observation

It was obtained from the Table 4.6.19 that the mean scores of Flexibility (V.C) of High group SES girls and Low group SES girls were 17.71 and 14.23 respectively. The obtained 't'-value was 2.515 at 0.013 level of significance.

Interpretation

The High group SES was greater than the Low group SES in mean score of Flexibility (V.C). And the obtained 't'-value was significant at 0.05 level of significance. In other words, the High group SES girls was advanced to the Low group SES girls in Flexibility of verbal creativity.

Observation

It was found from the Table 4.6.20 that the mean scores of Flexibility (N.V.C.) of High group SES and Low group SES were 14.56 and 12.54 respectively. The mean difference was 2.019 between them. The obtained 't'-value was 2.211 at 0.029 level of significance.

Interpretation

From the Table 4.6.20, the obtained 't'-value ($t = 2.211$, $df = 102$, $p < 0.05$) was significant at 0.05 level of significance with df = 102. Here, also, the High group SES was superior to the Low group SES in mean score of Flexibility of non-verbal creativity.

From the earlier discussions, it might be interpreted that the High group SES girls was significantly superior to the Low group SES girls in Flexibility of verbal creativity as well as that of non-verbal creativity.

Table - 4.6.19: Showing Significance of the Difference Between Means of Flexibility (V.C) for High and Low Groups Socio-economic Status Girls

Component	*Group*	*N*	*Mean*	*SD*	*SEm*	*MD*	*SED*	*t*	*df*	*Sig. (2-tailed)*
Fx_V.C	High	52	17.71	7.947	1.102	3.481	1.384	2.515	102	0.013
	Low	52	14.23	6.035	0.837					

Table - 4.6.20: Showing Significance of the Difference Between Means of Flexibility (N.V.C.) for High and Low Groups Socio-economic Status Girls

Component	*Group*	*N*	*Mean*	*SD*	*SEm*	*MD*	*SED*	*t*	*df*	*Sig. (2-tailed)*
Fx_N.V.C	High	52	14.56	4.309	0.598	2.019	0.913	2.211	102	0.029
	Low	52	12.54	4.980	0.691					

4.6.3.2.3 Originality Component and High & Low Socio-economic Status Groups Girls

Observation

One-way ANOVA, from Table - 4.6.17 showed that the obtained F-values of Originality component of both verbal and non-verbal creativity were 11.690 at 0.001 level of significance and 7.551 at 0.007 level of significance respectively for High and Low groups SES girls.

Interpretation

The obtained F-values of Originality component of both verbal and non-verbal creativity were highly significant both at 0.01 level of significance with df = 1 and 102. Between the two groups - High & Low SES girls, which was superior to another, to know that further 't'-test had been applied.

Observation

The Table - 4.6.21 revealed that the mean scores of Originality (V.C) of High group and Low group SES girls were 38.54 and 29.54 respectively and the mean difference was 9.000. The obtained 't'-value was 3.419 at 0.001 level of significance with df = 102.

Interpretation

The High group SES girls significantly differed from the Low group SES girls in Originality of Verbal Creativity and the High group SES was advanced to the Low group.

Observation

It was obtained from the Table - 4.6.2.2 that the mean scores of Originality component of non-verbal creativity (Or_N.V.C) of High group and Low group SES girls were 29.96 and 23.98 and the mean difference between them was 5.981. The obtained 't' value was 2.748 at 0.007 level of significance.

Interpretation

It might be implied from Table-4.6.22 that the obtained 't'-value

Table - 4.6.21: Showing Significance of the Difference Between Means of Originality (V. C.) for High and Low Groups Socio-economic Status Girls

Component	*Group*	*N*	*Mean*	*SD*	*SEm*	*MD*	*SED*	*t*	*df*	*Sig. (2-tailed)*
Or_V.C	High	52	38.54	15.367	2.131	9.000	2.632	3.419	102	0.001
	Low	52	29.54	11.143	1.545	a				

Table - 4.6.22: Showing Significance of the Difference Between Means of Originality (N.V.C) for High and Low Groups Socio-economic Status Girls

Component	*Group*	*N*	*Mean*	*SD*	*SEm*	*MD*	*SED*	*t*	*df*	*Sig. (2-tailed)*
Or_N.V.C	High	52	29.96	12.438	1.725	5.981	2.176	2.748	102	0.007
	Low	52	23.98	9.572	1.327					

was significant at 0.01 level of significance and the High group SES girls was superior to the Low group SES girls in Originality of non-verbal creativity.

Observation

It was obtained from the Table - 4.6.2.2 that the mean scores of Originality component of non-verbal creativity (Or_N.V.C) of High group and Low group SES girls were 29.96 and 23.98 and the mean difference between them was 5.981. The obtained 't' value was 2.748 at 0.007 level of significance.

Interpretation

It might be implied from Table-4.6.22 that the obtained 't'-value was significant at 0.01 level of significance and the High group SES girls was superior to the Low group SES girls in Originality of non-verbal creativity.

Hence, it might be interpreted that the High group SES girls was significantly advanced to the Low group SES girls in originality component of both verbal and non-verbal creativity.

From the discussions as mentioned in the sections 4.6.3.2.1; 4.6.3.2.2 and 4.6.3.2.3, one could conclude that the High group SES girls was significantly superior to the Low group SES girls in Fluency (verbal creativity), in Flexibility (both verbal and non-verbal creativity), in Originality (both verbal and non-verbal creativity). But there was no significant difference between the above two groups only in Fluency of non-verbal creativity. So, there was significant difference between High and Low Socio-economic Status groups girls in Fluency (Verbal), Flexibility and Originality scores. Hence, the hypothesis - H8 was accepted.

PART - V

CORRELATION TECHNIQUES AND REGRESSION ANALYSIS

4.7 Correlation Techniques

One of the main objectives of the present study is to find out the relationship between the components of creativity (with verbal and non-verbal) viz., Fluency, Flexibility, Originality and Independent Variables viz., Freedom, Socio-economic Status for boys and girls separately. The researcher followed the Pearson's Correlation Method in order to find out the relationship between them. The coefficients of correlation are interpreted at 5% and 1% level of significance (2-tailed) by using SPSS software version 12.0. For testing these hypotheses, the following findings and interpretations are given below:

4.7.1 Correlation between Freedom and Creativity

Students who enjoyed high freedom of thought and actions in the family, may have high creative thinking. So, creativity may be highly correlated with freedom of the students.

4.7.1.1 Correlation between Components of Creativity and Freedom enjoyed by the Boys in the Families

H_9: There would be significant relationship between Freedom of students and components of creativity (Fluency, Flexibility, Originality) of both verbal and non-verbal creativity tests for Boys.

Table- 4.7.1: Showing the Relationship between Freedom and Fluency of Verbal Creativity for Boys

Variable		*Fu_V.C*
Freedom	Pearson Correlation	0.284**
	Sig. (2-tailed)	0.000
	N	179

** Correlation is significant at the 0.01 level (2-tailed).

The above table showed that Pearson's Correlation value between Freedom enjoyed by the boys in the families and Fluency of Verbal Creativity was 0.284 which was significant at 0.01 level of significance. This indicated that there was a significant relationship between Freedom and Fluency of Verbal Creativity.

Table- 4.7.2: Showing the Relationship between Freedom and Fluency of Non-verbal Creativity for Boys

Variable		*Fu_N.V.C*
Freedom	Pearson Correlation	0.224**
	Sig. (2-tailed)	0.003
	N	179

** Correlation is significant at the 0.01 level (2-tailed).

The above table indicated that there was a positive correlation (0.224) between Freedom and Fluency of non-verbal creativity, which was significant at 0.01 level of significance. Thus, it might be concluded that there was a significant relationship between Freedom enjoyed by the Boys in the families and Fluency scores as obtained by the Boys in non-verbal creativity tests.

Table - 4.7.3: Showing the Relationship between Freedom and Flexibility of Verbal Creativity for Boys

Variable		*Fu_N.V.C*
Freedom	Pearson Correlation	0.242**
	Sig. (2-tailed)	0.001
	N	179

** Correlation is significant at the 0.01 level (2-tailed).

The above table showed that the co-efficient of correlation was 0.242 which was significant at 0.01 level of significance. That meant, the relationship between Freedom enjoyed by the boys in the families and Flexibility of Verbal Creativity was significant.

Table-4.7.4: Showing the Relationship between Freedom and Flexibility of Non-verbal Creativity for Boys

Variable		*Fu_N.V.C*
Freedom	Pearson Correlation	0.203**
	Sig. (2-tailed)	0.006
	N	179

** Correlation is significant at the 0.01 level (2-tailed).

The above table revealed that the Pearson's correlation value was 0.203 which was significant at 0.01 level of significance. It indicated that there was a significant positive relationship between Freedom of boys and Flexibility of Non-Verbal Creativity.

Table - 4.7.5: Showing the Relationship between Freedom and Originality of Verbal Creativity for Boys

Variable		*Or_V.C*
Freedom	Pearson Correlation	0.328**
	Sig. (2-tailed)	0.000
	N	179

** Correlation is significant at the 0.01 level (2-tailed).

The Table-4.7.5 indicated that there was a highly significant correlation between Freedom of students and Originality of verbal creativity. The correlation coefficient was significant at 0.01 level of significance.

Table - 4.7.6: Showing the Relationship between Freedom and Originality of Non-verbal Creativity for Boys

Variable		*Or_N.V.C*
Freedom	Pearson Correlation	0.131#
	Sig. (2-tailed)	0.082
	N	179

Correlation is not significant at the 0.05 level (2-tailed).

The above table showed that the obtained coefficient of correlation (0.131) was not significant even at 0.05 level of significance. It indicated that there was no significant relationship between the Freedom enjoyed by the boys in the families and Originality of non-verbal creativity.

From the earlier interpretations, it could be concluded that the Freedom enjoyed by the boys in the families was significantly correlated with Fluency (both verbal and non-verbal creativity), Flexibility (both verbal and non-verbal creativity), Originality (verbal). But there was no significant relationship between Freedom of boys and Originality of non-verbal creativity. Hence, the hypothesis H_9 might be accepted. That meant, there were significant relationships between Freedom of boys and components of creativity (verbal and non-verbal).

4.7.1.2.1 Correlation between Components of Verbal Creativity and Freedom enjoyed by the Girls in the Families

H_{10}: There would be significant relationship between Freedom of students and components of verbal creativity (Fluency, Flexibility, Originality) for girls.

Table - 4.7.7: Showing the Relationship between Freedom and Fluency of Verbal Creativity for Girls

Variable		*Fu_V.C*
Freedom	Pearson Correlation	0.149*
	Sig. (2-tailed)	0.038
	N	193

*Correlation is significant at the 0.05 level (2-tailed).

The above table showed that the Pearson's correlation value was 0.149 which was significant at 0.05 level of significance. It indicated that there was a significant relationship between Freedom enjoyed by the girls in the families and Fluency of Verbal Creativity.

Table - 4.7.8: Showing the Relationship between Freedom and Flexibility of Verbal Creativity for Girls

Variable		*Fx_V.C*
Freedom	Pearson Correlation	0.140#
	Sig. (2-tailed)	0.053
	N	193

Correlation is not significant at the 0.05 level (2-tailed).

It was to be noted from the above table that the obtained coefficient of correlation was 0.140 which was not significant even at 0.05 level of significance. Thus, there was no significant relationship between the Freedom enjoyed by the girls in the families and the Flexibility of Verbal Creativity.

Table - 4.7.9: Showing the Relationship between Freedom and Originality of Verbal Creativity for Girls

Variable		*Or_V.C*
Freedom	Pearson Correlation	0.243**
	Sig. (2-tailed)	0.001
	N	193

** Correlation is significant at the 0.01 level (2-tailed).

It was seen from Table-4.7.9 that there was a significant positive correlation between Freedom scores and Originality scores (V.C.). The correlation was significant at 0.01 level of significance. It indicated that there was a significant relationship between Freedom enjoyed by the girls of the families and the Originality component of verbal creativity.

From the earlier three interpretations it might be concluded that the Freedom of the girls in the families was significantly correlated with Fluency and Originality components of verbal creativity but not correlated with Flexibility component. Hence, the hypothesis H_{10} was mostly true. Thus, the hypothesis might be accepted.

4.7.1.2.2 Correlation between Components of Non-verbal Creativity and Freedom enjoyed by the Girls in the Families

H_{11}: There would be significant relationship between Freedom of students and components of non-verbal creativity (Fluency, Flexibility, Originality) for girls.

Table - 4.7.10: Showing the Relationship between Freedom and Fluency of Non-verbal Creativity for Girls

Variable		*Fu_N.V.C*
Freedom	Pearson Correlation	0.108#
	Sig. (2-tailed)	0.134
	N	193

Correlation is not significant at the 0.05 level (2-tailed).

The above table showed that the obtained co-efficient of correlation (0.108) was not significant even at 0.05 level of significance. It implied that there was no significant relationship between the Freedom enjoyed by the girls in the families and Fluency of non-verbal creativity.

Table - 4.7.11: Showing the Relationship between Freedom and Flexibility of Non-verbal Creativity for Girls

Variable		*Fx_N.V.C*
Freedom	Pearson Correlation	0.094#
	Sig. (2-tailed)	0.192
	N	193

Correlation is not significant at the 0.05 level (2-tailed).

It was seen from the Table 4.7.11 that the coefficient of correlation between Freedom and Flexibility (Fx_N.V.C) was 0.094 which was not significant even at 0.05 level of significant. That meant, there was no significant relationship between Freedom enjoyed by the girls in the family and Flexibility of non-verbal creativity.

Table - 4.7.12: Showing the Relationship between Freedom and Originality of Non-verbal Creativity for Girls

Variable		*Or_N.V.C*
Freedom	Pearson Correlation	0.137#
	Sig. (2-tailed)	0.058
	N	193

Correlation is not significant at the 0.05 level (2-tailed).

It was to be noted from the above Table-4.7.12 that the Pearson Correlation value (0.137) was not significant even at 0.05 level of significance. It indicated that there was no significant relationship between Freedom enjoyed by the girls in the families and Originality of non-verbal creativity.

From the earlier three interpretations, it could be concluded that the Freedom enjoyed by the girl students in the families was not significantly correlated with Fluency, Flexibility and Originality of non-verbal creativity. In other words, there was no significant relationship between Freedom of girl students and the components of non-verbal creativity. So, the hypothesis - H_{11} was totally rejected.

4.7.2 Correlation between Socio-economic Status and Creativity

Socio-economic Status (SES) may be positively correlated with the creativity. Students of the family of high Socio-economic Status may have more scores in various components of creativity for getting the enriched family environment. On the other hand, the students of Low Socio-economic Status may get low scores in the components of creativity.

4.7.2.1.1 Correlation between Components of Verbal Creativity and Socio-economic Status of the Family for Boys:

H_{12}: There would be significant relationship between Socio-economic Status and components of verbal creativity (Fluency, Flexibility, Originality) for boys.

Table - 4.7.13: Showing the Relationship between Socio-economic Status and Fluency of Verbal Creativity for Boys

Variable		*Fu_V.C*
S. E. Status	Pearson Correlation	0.047#
	Sig. (2-tailed)	0.535
	N	179

Correlation is not significant at the 0.05 level (2-tailed).

The above table showed that the co-efficient of correlation was 0.047 which was not significant at 0.05 level of significance. It indicated that the relationship between Socio-economic Status and Fluency of Verbal Creativity was not significant even at 0.05 level of significance.

Table - 4.7.14: Showing the Relationship between Socio-economic Status and Flexibility of Verbal Creativity for Boys

Variable		*Fx_V.C*
S. E. Status	Pearson Correlation	0.002#
	Sig. (2-tailed)	0.984
	N	179

#Correlation is not significant at the 0.05 level (2-tailed).

It was found from Table-4.7.14 that the Pearson correlation value was very low. It indicated that the relationship between socio-economic status of the families of boys and Flexibility of verbal creativity was not significant even at 0.05 level of significance.

Table - 4.7.15: Showing the Relationship between Socio-economic Status and Originality of Verbal Creativity for Boys

Variable		*Or_V.C*
S. E. Status	Pearson Correlation	0.073#
	Sig. (2-tailed)	0.334
	N	179

#Correlation is not significant at the 0.05 level (2-tailed).

The above table showed that the obtained co-efficient of correlation (0.073) was positive but not significant at 0.05 level of significance. It implied that the relationship between socio-economic status of the boys' families and Originality component of verbal creativity was not significant even at 0.05 level of significance.

From the earlier three interpretations, it could be concluded that the Socio-economic Status of the boys' families was not significantly correlated with the components of verbal creativity viz.; Fluency, Flexibility and Originality. That meant, there was no significant relationship between socio-economic status and components of verbal creativity. So, the hypothesis - H_{12} was totally rejected.

4.7.2.1.2 Correlation between Components of Non-verbal Creativity and Socio-economic Status of the Family for Boys

H_{13}: There would be significant relationship between Socio-economic Status and components of non-verbal creativity (Fluency, Flexibility, Originality) for boys.

Table - 4.7.16: Showing the Relationship between Socio-economic Status and Fluency of Non-verbal Creativity for Boys

Variable		*Fu_N.V.C*
S. E. Status	Pearson Correlation	0.143#
	Sig. (2-tailed)	0.056
	N	179

#Correlation is not significant at the 0.05 level (2-tailed).

It was to be noted from the above Table-4.7.16 that the coefficient of correlation (0.143) was not significant even at 0.05 level of significance. It indicated that there was no significant relationship between socio-economic status of the families of the boys and Fluency of non-verbal creativity.

Table - 4.7.17: Showing the Relationship between Socio-economic Status and Flexibility of Non-verbal Creativity for Boys

Variable		*Fx_N.V.C*
S. E. Status	Pearson Correlation	0.169*
	Sig. (2-tailed)	0.024
	N	179

*Correlation is significant at the 0.05 level (2-tailed).

The above table showed that Pearson's Correlation Value (0.169) was positive and significant at 0.05 level of significance. That meant, Socio-economic Status of the families of boys and Flexibility of non-verbal creativity were positively correlated and the relationship between them was significant at 0.05 level of significance.

Table - 4.7.18: Showing the Relationship between Socio-economic Status and Originality of Non-verbal Creativity for Boys

Variable		*Or_N.V.C*
S. E. Status	Pearson Correlation	0.258**
	Sig. (2-tailed)	0.000
	N	179

**Correlation is not significant at the 0.01 level (2-tailed).

The Table-4.7.18 showed that the coefficient of correlation (0.258) was highly significant at 0.01 level of significance. It indicated that the relationship between Socio-economic Status of the families and Originality of Non-verbal Creativity was highly significant.

From the earlier three interpretations, it might be concluded that the Socio-economic Status of the boys' families was significantly correlated with Flexibility and Originality but not significantly correlated with Fluency. Hence the hypothesis (H_{13}) might be accepted.

4.7.2.2 Correlation between Components of Creativity and Socio-economic Status of the Family for Girls

H_{14}: There would be significant relationship between Socio-economic Status and components of creativity (Fluency, Flexibility,

Originality) of both verbal and non-verbal creativity tests for girls.

Table - 4.7.19: Showing the Relationship between Socio-economic Status and Fluency of Verbal Creativity for Girls

Variable		*Fu_V.C*
S. E. Status	Pearson Correlation	0.222**
	Sig. (2-tailed)	0.002
	N	193

**Correlation is not significant at the 0.01 level (2-tailed).

The above table showed that Pearson's Correlation value was 0.222 which was significant at 0.01 level of significance. It indicated that the socio-economic status of the families of girls was significantly related with Fluency of verbal creativity.

Table - 4.7.20: Showing the Relationship between Socio-economic Status and Fluency of Non-verbal Creativity for Girls

Variable		*Fu_N.V.C*
S. E. Status	Pearson Correlation	0.064#
	Sig. (2-tailed)	0.374
	N	193

#Correlation is not significant at the 0.05 level (2-tailed).

It was obtained from Table-4.7.20 that the coefficient of correlation was 0.064 which was not significant even at 0.05 level of significance. That meant, the Socio-economic Status of the girls' families was not significantly related with Fluency of non-verbal creativity.

Table - 4.7.21: Showing the Relationship between Socio-economic Status and Flexibility of Verbal Creativity for Girls

Variable		*Fx_V.C*
S. E. Status	Pearson Correlation	0.245**
	Sig. (2-tailed)	0.001
	N	193

**Correlation is significant at the 0.01 level (2-tailed).

The above table showed that the relationship between Socio-economic Status of the families of girls and Flexibility of Verbal Creativity was positive and significant at 0.01 level of significance.

Table - 4.7.22: Showing the Relationship between Socio-economic Status and Flexibility of Non-verbal Creativity for Girls

Variable		*Fx_N.V.C*
S. E. Status	Pearson Correlation	0.149*
	Sig. (2-tailed)	0.039
	N	193

*Correlation is significant at the 0.05 level (2-tailed).

The above table showed that the correlation value was 0.149 which was significant at 0.05 level of significance. It indicated that the relationship between Socio-economic Status of the girls' families and Flexibility of non-verbal creativity was positive and significant.

Table - 4.7.23: Showing the Relationship between Socio-economic Status and Originality of Verbal Creativity for Girls

Variable		*Or_V.C*
S. E. Status	Pearson Correlation	0.322**
	Sig. (2-tailed)	0.000
	N	193

**Correlation is significant at the 0.01 level (2-tailed).

The above table showed that the correlation value was 0.322 which was significant at 0.01 level of significance. It indicated that the socio-economic status of the girls' families was positively correlated with Originality of verbal creativity and the relation was significant.

Table - 4.7.24: Showing the Relationship between Socio-economic Status and Originality of Non-verbal Creativity for Girls

Variable		*Or_N.V.C*
S. E. Status	Pearson Correlation	0.237**
	Sig. (2-tailed)	0.001
	N	193

**Correlation is significant at the 0.01 level (2-tailed).

The above table indicated that the relationship between Socio-economic Status of the families of the girls and Originality of non-verbal creativity was positive and also significant at 0.01 level of significance.

From the earlier six interpretations, it could be concluded that Socio-economic Status of the families of the girls was significantly correlated with Fluency (verbal), Flexibility (verbal and non-verbal), Originality (verbal and non-verbal) components of Creativity. Only Fluency of non-verbal creativity was not significantly correlated with socio-economic status of the families of girls. That meant, it might be said that there was a significant positive relationship between Socio-economic Status of the families of the girls and components of both verbal and non-verbal creativity. Hence, the formulated hypothesis- H14 was accepted.

4.8 Regression Analysis

The most useful approach to the prediction of dependent variable(s) from a set of independent variables was step-wise multiple regression. One specific advantage of the application of step-wise multiple regression analysis was the possibility of valuating the relative contribution of the set of independent variables to the variance in the dependent variable. This would provide a picture of nature and extent to which independent variables were involved in predicting the dependent variable. The multiple regression equation used here was as follows:

$$\hat{Y} = a + \beta_1 X_1 + \beta_2 X_2 + \beta_3 X_3 + \ldots\ldots\ldots\ldots + \beta_n X_n$$

where Y denotes the outcome variable and may be predicted from a linear combination of the scores on different independent variables (X1, X2, X3, ...Xn) multiplied with their beta coefficients and intercept or constant (a) of the regression line.

In the present study, the researcher applied step-wise multiple regression procedure on three predictor variables (Freedom of the students, Socio-economic Status) to predict-

i) Total Fluency,

ii) Total Flexibility,

iii) Total Originality.

4.8.1 Total Fluency of Creativity

A) Inter-correlation

Table - 4.8.1: Inter-correlations among Total Fluency, Freedom, Socio-economic Status

Variable	*Variable*	*N*	*Pearson Correlation*	*Sig. (1-tailed)*
Fu_TOTAL	Freedom	372	0.231	0.000**
Fu_TOTAL	S.E.Status	372	0.146	0.002**
Freedom	S.E.Status	372	0.192	0.000**

**Correlation is significant at the 0.01 level and *Correlation is significant at the 0.05 level (1-tailed).

The above table showed that Freedom of the students was highly correlated with Total Fluency as the correlation value was 0.231 which was significant at 0.01 level of significance. And Socio-economic Status was significantly correlated with Total Fluency at 0.01 level of significance. The inter-correlation coefficient between Freedom and Socio-economic Status was 0.192. The relationship was significant at 0.01 level of significance.

B) Analysis and Formulation of Regression Equation

In this analysis, Total Fluency of all the students (Total sample - both Boys and Girls; 372) was treated as the dependent or outcome variable and their scores on Freedom and Socio-economic Status were independent or predictor variables. Total Fluency was obtained by adding the Fluency of verbal creativity and Fluency of non-verbal creativity after converting them into T-scores separately (Appendix - B). Step-wise multiple regression analysis was carried out to find out the maximum possible variance in Total Fluency of all the students that could be explained with the help of each of the independent variables. Results of the step-wise multiple regression had been presented in the Table-4.8.2 and Table-4.8.3.

Table-4.8.2: Summary of the Step-wise Multiple Regression Model for Dependent Variable: Total Fluency

Model	*R*	*R Square*	*Adjusted R Square*	*F-value*	*Signifi-cance*	*Durbin Watson Value*
1	0.231a	0.053	0.051	20.871	0.000	1.404
2	0.253b	0.064	0.059	12.634	0.000	

a = Predictors : (Constant), Freedom

b = Predictors : (Constant), Freedom, S. E. Status

(1) Model: 1 (Predictor: Freedom)

From the Table-4.8.2 and Table-4.8.3, it was seen that the first variable entered in the step-wise multiple regression analysis was Freedom. The multiple correlation (R) obtained about 0.231. The value indicated that the strength of the relationship between two variables was about 23.1%. The F-ratio for the first model was highly significant [$F = 20.871$ and $p < 0.001$]. One could interpret this result as the first model which would significantly improve the ability to predict the outcome variable (Total Fluency).

The co-efficient of multiple R square (R2) was 0.053. This showed that 5.30% of the variance on Total Fluency was accounted by Freedom. Moreover, the Adjusted R square was 0.051 and the difference between R2 and adjusted R2 was (0.053 - 0.051) = 0.002 (about 0.2%). This shrinkage meant that if the model were derived from the population rather than a sample it would be accounted for approximately 0.2% less variance in the outcome.

The standard error of the estimate for the model was 0.212 and Durbin-Watson Value was 1.404 which lied between 1 and 3, the t-value was highly significant ($t = 4.569$, $p < 0.001$), it revealed that the value differed significantly from zero. In other words, the predictor was making a significant contribution to the model. The constant or intercept value that was considered in the equation at the end of the first step, with which prediction of Total Fluency would be possible,

Table - 4.8.3: Step-wise Multiple Regression of Dependent Variable: Total Fluency (Fu_TOTAL) with Predictor Variables

Model	Predictor Variables	Constant	Unstandardized Coefficients		Standardized Coefficients	t-value	Sig.	Correlations		Percentage of Variance
			β	Std. Error	Beta			Zero Order	Partial	
1	Freedom	84.745	0.969	0.212	0.231	4.569	0.000	0.231	0.231	5.34
2	Freedom S. E. Status	82.186 –	0.884 0.050	0.215 0.024	0.211 0.105	4.110 2.053	0.000 0.041	0.231 0.146	0.209 0.106	4.87 1.53

was 84.745. Thus, the multiple regression equation at the end of this first step would be as follows:

Fu_TOTAL = 84.745 + 0.969 (Freedom)....................(1)

(2) Model: 2 (Predictors: Freedom, S. E. Status):

The next predictor variable entered in the second step was Socio-economic Status (S. E. Status). The multiple correlation obtained between Total Fluency and two predictor variables viz. Freedom and S. E. Status was 0.253. The multiple R2 was 0.064. It revealed that the two variables put together could explain about 6.4% of the variance in the outcome variable (Total Fluency). From the 6.4% of the variance, Freedom explained 4.87% of variance and S. E. Status contributed 1.53% of variance. The F-value for the second model was also highly significant [$F = 12.634$, $p < 0.001$].

It could be seen that, by the inclusion of Socio-economic Status, the contribution of Freedom had been brought down from 5.30% to 4.87% due to inter-correlation between the two predictor variables. The t-values of these two variables were also highly significant ($p < 0.001$ and $p < 0.05$ respectively). In this step the regression equation would be as follows:

Fu_TOTAL = 82.186 + 0.884 (Freedom) + 0.050 (S. E. Status).....(2)

Freedom appeared to be the relatively greater contributing factor in Total Fluency of Creativity. Next, contributing factors were Socio-economic Status.

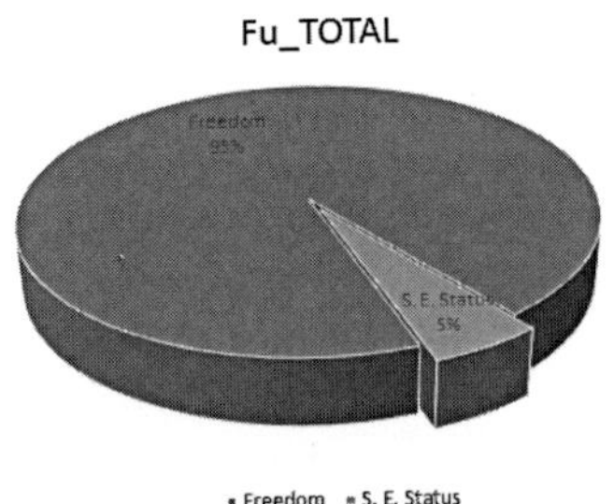

Fig. 4.8.1: Relative Contribution (Percentage) of the Predictor Variables to Total Fluency of Creativity

C) β-value Analysis

The calculation of -values was important because they would explain the relationship between Total Fluency and each predictor. Positive value represented the positive relationship between predictor and the outcome. When the two predictor variables (Freedom and Socio-economic Status) were increased, the Total Fluency would also increase. Apart from these, -values expressed the degrees of each predictor effect on the outcome when the effects of other predictors were held constant.

Freedom (β = 0.884):

This value indicated that when Freedom increased by one-unit, Total Fluency would increase by 0.884 unit. This interpretation was true only when the effect of Socio-economic Status was held constant.

Socio-economic Status (β = 0.050)

This value indicated that the increase of S. E. Status by one unit, the outcome variable - Total Fluency would increase by 0.050 unit. This interpretation was true only when the effect of Freedom was held constant.

4.8.2 Total Flexibility of Creativity

A) Inter-correlation

Table-4.8.4: Inter-correlations among Total Flexibility, Freedom, Socio-economic Status

Variable	*Variable*	*N*	*Pearson Correlation*	*Sig. (1-tailed)*
Fx_TOTAL	Freedom	372	0.210	0.000**
Fx_TOTAL	S.E.Status	372	0.180	0.000**
Freedom	S.E.Status	372	0.192	0.000**

**Correlation is significant at the 0.01 level and *Correlation is significant at the 0.05 level (1-tailed)

#Correlation is not significant at the 0.05 level (1-tailed).

The above table showed that Freedom of the students was highly correlated with Total Flexibility as the correlation value was 0.210 which was significant at 0.01 level of significance. And Socio-economic Status was also significantly correlated with Total Flexibility at 0.01 level of significance. The inter-correlation coefficient between Freedom and Socio-economic Status was 0.192. The relationship was significant at 0.01 level of significance.

B) Analysis and Formulation of Regression Equation

In this analysis, Total Flexibility of all the students (Total sample - both Boys and girls; 372) was treated as the dependent or outcome variable and their scores on Freedom and Socio-economic Status were independent or predictor variables. Total Flexibility was obtained by adding the Flexibility of verbal creativity and Flexibility of non-verbal creativity after converting them into T-scores separately (Appendix - B). Step-wise multiple regression analysis was carried out to find out the maximum possible variance in Total Flexibility of all the students that could be explained with the help of each of the independent variables. Results of the step-wise multiple regression had been presented in the Table-4.8.5 and Table-4.8.6.

Table - 4.8.5: Summary of the Step-wise Multiple Regression Model for Dependent Variable: Total Flexibility

Model	*R*	*R Square*	*Adjusted R Square*	*F-value*	*Signifi-cance*	*Durbin Watson Value*
1	0.210a	0.044	0.041	17.006	0.000	1.417
2	0.253b	0.064	0.059	12.643	0.000	

a = Predictors : (Constant), Freedom

b = Predictors : (Constant), Freedom, S. E. Status

Table – 4.8.6: Step-wise Multiple Regression of Dependent Variable: Total Flexibility (Fx_TOTAL) with Predictor Variables

Model	Predictor Variables	Constant	Unstandardized Coefficients		Standardized Coefficients	t-value	Sig.	Correlations		Percentage of Variance
			β	Std. Error	Beta			Zero Order	Partial	
1	Freedom	86.460	0.860	0.208	0.210	4.124	0.000	0.210	0.210	4.41
2	Freedom S. E. Status	83.019 –	0.746 0.067	0.210 0.024	0.182 0.145	3.544 2.822	0.000 0.005	0.210 0.180	0.181 0.145	3.82 2.61

(1) Model: 1 (Predictor: Freedom)

From the Table-4.8.5 and Table-4.8.6 it was seen that the first variable entered in the step-wise multiple regression analysis was Freedom. The multiple correlation (R) obtained about 0.210. The value indicated that the strength of the relationship between two variables was about 21.0%. The F-ratio for the first model was highly significant [F = 17.006, and $p < 0.001$]. One could interpret this result as the first model which would be significant improve the ability to predict the outcome variable (Total Flexibility).

The co-efficient of multiple R square (R2) was 0.044. This showed that 4.40% of the variance on Total Flexibility was accounted by Freedom. Moreover, the Adjusted R square was 0.041 and the difference between R2 and adjusted R2 was (0.044 - 0.041) = 0.003 (about 0.3%). This shrinkage meant that if the model were derived from the population rather than a sample it would be accounted for approximately 0.3% less variance in the outcome.

The standard error of the estimate for the model was 0.208 and Durbin-Watson value was 1.417 which lied between 1 and 3, and the t-value was highly significant (t = 4.124, $p < 0.001$), it revealed that the -value differed significantly from zero. In other words, the predictor was making a significant contribution to the model. The constant or intercept value that was considered in the equation at the end of the first step, with which prediction of Total Flexibility would be possible, was 86.460. Thus, the multiple regression equation at the end of this first step would be as follows:

Fx_TOTAL = 86.460 + 0.860 (Freedom)..................(1)

(2) Model: 2 (Predictors: Freedom, S. E. Status):

The next predictor variable entered in the second step was Socio-economic Status (S. E. Status). The multiple correlation obtained between Total Flexibility and two predictor variables, viz., Freedom and S. E. Status was 0.253. The multiple R2 was 0.064. It revealed that the two variables put together could explain about 6.4% of the variance in the outcome variable (Total Flexibility). From this 6.4% of the variance, Freedom explained 3.82% of variance and S. E.

Status contributed 2.61% of variance. The F-value for the second model was also highly significant [$F = 12.634$, $p < 0.001$].

It could be seen that, by the inclusion of Socio-economic Status, the contribution of Freedom had been brought down from 4.41% to 3.82% due to inter-correlation between the two predictor variables. The t-values of these two variables were also highly significant ($p < 0.001$ and $p = 0.005$ respectively).

In this step the regression equation would be as follows:

Fx-TOTAL = 83.019 + 0.746 (Freedom) + 0.067 (S. E. Status)......(2)

Freedom appeared to be the relatively greater contributing factor in Total Flexibility of Creativity. Next contributing factor was Socio-economic Status.

Figure-4.8.2 showed the relative contribution of predictor variables on Total Flexibility of Creativity.

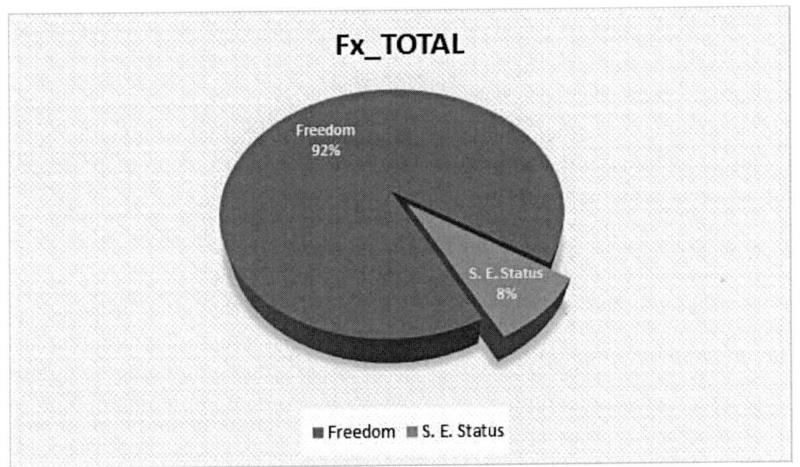

Fig. 4.8.2: Relative contribution (Percentage) of the Predictor Variables to Total Flexibility of Creativity

C) β-value Analysis

The calculation of -values was important because they would explain the relationship between Total Flexibility and each predictor. Positive -value represented the positive relationship between predictor and the outcome. When the two predictor variables (Freedom and Socio-economic Status) were increased, the Total Flexibility would also increase. Apart from these, -values expressed the degrees of each predictor effect on the outcome when the effects of other predictors were held constant.

Freedom (β= 0.746)

This value indicated that when Freedom increased by one-unit, Total Flexibility would increase by 0.746 unit. This interpretation was true only when the effects of socio-economic status was held constant.

Socio-economic Status (β= 0.067)

This value indicated that the increase of S. E. Status by one unit, the outcome variable - Total Flexibility would increase by 0.067 unit. This interpretation was true only when the effect of Freedom was held constant.

4.8.3 Total Originality of Creativity

A) Inter-correlation

Table-4.8.7: Inter-correlations among Total Originality, Socio-economic Status, Freedom

Variable	*Variable*	*N*	*Pearson Correlation*	*Sig. (1-tailed)*
Or_TOTAL	Freedom	372	0.277	0.000**
Or_TOTAL	S.E.Status	372	0.257	0.000**
Freedom	S.E.Status	372	0.192	0.000**

**Correlation is significant at the 0.01 level and *Correlation is significant at the 0.05 level (1-tailed)

The above table showed that Socio-economic Status of the families was highly correlated with Total Originality as the correlation value was 0.277 which was significant at 0.01 level of significance. And Freedom was also significantly correlated with Total Originality at 0.01 level of significance. The inter-correlation coefficient between Socio-economic status and Freedom was 0.192. The relationship was significant at 0.01.

B) Analysis and Formulation of Regression Equation

In this analysis, Total Originality of all the students (Total sample - both Boys and Girls; 372) was treated as the dependent or outcome variable and their scores on Socio-economic Status and Freedom were independent or predictor variables. Total Originality was obtained by adding the Originality of verbal creativity and Originality of non-verbal creativity after converting them into T-scores separately (Appendix -B). Step-wise multiple regression analysis was carried out to find out the maximum possible variance in Total Originality of all the students that could be explained with the help of each of the independent variables. Results of the step-wise regression had been presented in the Table-4.8.8 and Table-4.8.9.

Table-4.8.8: Summary of the Step-wise Multiple Regression Model for Dependent Variable: Total Originality

Model	*R*	*R Square*	*Adjusted R Square*	*F-value*	*Signifi-cance*	*Durbin Watson Value*
1	0.277a	0.077	0.074	30.762	0.000	1.431
2	0.347b	0.120	0.115	25.176	0.000	

a = Predictors: (Constant), S. E. Status

b = Predictors: (Constant), Freedom, S. E. Status

Table - 4.8.9: Step-wise Multiple Regression of Dependent Variable: Total Originality (Or_TOTAL) with Predictor Variables

Model	Predictor Variables	Constant	Unstandardized Coefficients		Standardized Coefficients	t-value	Sig.	Correlations		Percentage of Variance
			β	Std. Error	Beta			Zero Order	Partial	
1	S. E. Status	89.890	0.129	0.023	0.277	5.546	0.000	0.277	0.277	7.67
2	S. E. Status Freedom	77.547 –	0.110 0.878	0.023 0.206	0.236 0.212	4.751 4.262	0.000 0.000	0.277 0.257	0.240 0.217	6.54 5.45

(1) Model 1 (Predictor: S. E. Status)

From the Table-4.8.8 and Table-4.8.9 it was seen that the first variable entered in the step-wise multiple regression analysis was socio-economic status. The multiple correlation (R) obtained 0.277. The value indicated that the strength of the relationship between two variables was 27.7%. The F-ratio for the first model was highly significant [$F = 30.762$, and $p < 0.001$]. One could interpret this result as the first model which would significantly improve the ability to predict the outcome variable (Total Originality).

The co-efficient of multiple R square (R2) was 0.077. This showed that 7.70% of the variance on Total Originality was accounted by S. E. Status. Moreover, the Adjusted R square was 0.074 and the difference between R2 and adjusted R2 was (0.077 - 0.074) = 0.003 (about 0.3%). This shrinkage meant that if the model were derived from the population rather than a sample it would be accounted for approximately 0.3% less variance in the outcome.

The standard error of the estimate for the model was 0.023 and Durbin-Watson value was 1.431 which lied between 1 and 3, the t-value was highly significant [$t = 5.546$, $p < 0.001$], it revealed that the -value differed significantly from zero. In other words, the predictor was making a significant contribution to the model. The constant or intercept value that was considered in the equation at the end of the first step, with which prediction of Total Originality would be possible, was 89.890. Thus, the multiple regression equation at the end of this first step would be as follows:

Or_TOTAL = 89.890 + 0.129 (S. E. Status)........................(1)

(2) Model: 2 (Predictors: S. E. Status, Freedom)

The next predictor variable entered in the second step was Freedom. The multiple correlation obtained between Total Originality and two predictor variables viz.; Freedom and S. E. Status and Freedom was 0.347. The multiple R2 was 0.120. It revealed that the two variables put together could explain about 12.0% of the variance in the outcome variable (Total Originality). From this 12.0% of the variance, S. E. Status explained 6.54% of variance and Freedom contributed about 5.46% of variance. The F-value for the second model was also highly significant [$F = 25.176$, $p < 0.001$].

It could be seen that, by the inclusion of Freedom, the contribution of S. E. Status had been brought down from 7.67% to 6.54% due to inter-correlation between the two predictor variables. The t-values of these two variables were also highly significant ($p < 0.001$). In this step the regression equation would be as follows:

Or_TOTAL = 77.547 + 0.110 (S. E. Status) + 0.878 (Freedom)..................(2)

Freedom appeared to be the relatively greater contributing factor in Total Originality of creativity. Next contributing factor was Socio-economic Status.

Figure-4.8.3 showed the relative contribution of predictor variables on Total Originality of Creativity.

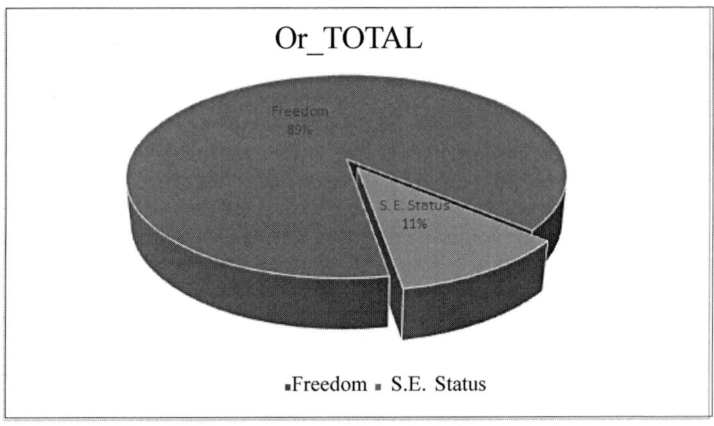

Fig. 4.8.3: Relative Contribution (Percentage) of the Predictor Variables to Total Originality of Creativity

C) β-value Analysis

The calculation of -values was important because they would explain the relationship between Total Originality and each predictor.

Positive -value represented the positive relationship between predictor and the outcome. When the two predictor variables (S. E. Status and Freedom) were increased, the Total Originality would also increase. Apart from these, values expressed the degrees of each predictor effect on the outcome when the effect of other predictor was held constant.

Socio-economic Status (β= 0.110)

This value indicated that when S. E. Status increased by one-unit, Total Originality would increase by 0.110 unit. This interpretation was true only when the effect of Freedom was held constant.

Freedom (β= 0.878)

This value indicated that the increase of Freedom by one unit, the outcome variable - Total Originality would increase by 0.878 unit. This interpretation was true only when the effect of S. E. Status was held constant.

5

FINDINGS AND DISCUSSIONS

On the basis of the graphical representation, the statistical analysis and interpretation made in the previous chapter (Chapter - IV), the researcher tried to mention the findings of the study very clearly and to discuss these findings to ascertain the extent to which these results might be useful in shedding light on the research problems raised in the first chapter and also to link them with the empirical findings in the specific areas with which the present investigation was concerned.

In this chapter various findings were mentioned together, obtained by applying different statistical techniques viz.; ANOVA, t-test, correlation etc. and were discussed in the light of the objectives of the study under the headings of independent variables (Gender, Freedom, Socio-economic Status) considered in the study. Again, the researcher tried to discuss the relative contribution of the independent variables to the components of creativity. At last of this chapter, the researcher intended to discuss about the ideal family environment for developing creativity among the children regarding the aspects considered in the study.

5.1 Creativity and Gender Difference

The present study aimed at to determine, whether there was any gender difference in different components viz., fluency, flexibility and originality of both verbal and non-verbal creativity. For this purpose, the present study included 372 students of class VIII and class IX as a sample, out of which 179 students were boys and 193 students were girls (Table: 3.2).

There were three hypotheses considered regarding gender difference in creativity in this study. They were in the three dimensions of creativity viz., fluency, flexibility and originality for both verbal and non-verbal creativity. These three hypotheses were mentioned and discussed below:

Hypothesis – H_1: There would be no significant difference between boys and girls in Fluency scores of verbal and non-verbal creativity.

This hypothesis was totally accepted. That meant, there was no significant difference between boys and girls in Fluency scores of both verbal and non-verbal creativity as found in the section 4.6.1.1.

The comparison between boys and girls in verbal Fluency and non-verbal Fluency had been shown by plotting Ogives as in the Figure 4.4.1 and Figure 4.4.2 separately. It was found from these graphical representations that boys were not so different from girls in both verbal and non-verbal fluency.

Hypothesis – H_2: There would be no significant difference between boys and girls in Flexibility scores of verbal and non-verbal creativity.

This hypothesis was rejected. This indicated that significant difference existed between boys and girls in flexibility scores of verbal and non-verbal creativity. But, in flexibility of verbal creativity girls were superior to boys and in flexibility of non-verbal creativity boys were advanced to girls (Section – 4.6.1.2).

Graphical representations as shown in the figures 4.4.3 and 4.4.4 also indicated that there were significant differences existed between boys and girls in both verbal and non-verbal flexibility.

Hypothesis – H_3: There would be no significant difference between boys and girls in Originality scores of verbal and non-verbal creativity.

This null hypothesis was accepted. That meant, there was no significant difference between boys and girls in Originality scores of both verbal and non-verbal creativity (Section – 4.6.1.3).

Graphical representation as shown in the Figures 4.4.5 and 4.4.6 also demanded that there was no significant difference existed between boys and girls in originality of both verbal and non-verbal creativity.

The description of fluency, flexibility and originality of both verbal and non-verbal creativity had been shown in the Table: 4.2.1 and Table: 4.2.3 for boys group and girls group respectively.

Findings

- There was no significant difference between boys and girls in Fluency and Originality components of both verbal and non-verbal creativity.
- In flexibility component of creativity, there were significant differences existed between boys and girls. Girls were superior to boys in verbal Flexibility but boys were advanced to girls in non-verbal Flexibility.

Discussion

The present study revealed that for both verbal and non-verbal creativity, gender was not a contributing factor to creativity and its components (except flexibility). Boys did not differ from girls in fluency scores and originality scores of both verbal and non-verbal creativity. But in flexibility of verbal creativity, girls were advanced to boys and in flexibility of non-verbal creativity boys were more advanced to girls. Overall, the gender difference was found not to be significant in creativity.

The above findings got support from Guilford and others (1961), Raina (1970), Passi (1972), Jain (1975), Sharma (1979), Dharmangadan (1981), Bhogayata (1986).

Also, Mukherjee, M. (2007) mentioned findings in her Ph. D. Thesis submitted to the University of Kalyani that boys did not differ from girls on the fluency, flexibility, originality and elaboration of both verbal and figural creativity.

But Raina (1971) and Goyal (1974) found that females were significantly superior to males only on fluency and flexibility dimensions of creativity and Singh (1978) reported that female students were superior to male students in fluency and originality dimensions of creativity.

Again, male students were found to be significantly superior to their female counterparts on verbal creativity as stated by Prakash (1966), Gagneja (1972), Jain (1975), Rawat and Agarwal (1977) and Sharma (1979).

In the present study the two groups - boys and girls were different only in flexibility scores. But for verbal or non-verbal creativity, one of the two groups exceeded another in flexibility. This indicated that in the dimension of flexibility, one group (boys or girls) could not demand absolute superior to another.

It might be concluded from the discussions that for both verbal and non-verbal creativity, the boys group had not absolute superiority with respect to the girls group in the dimensions of fluency, flexibility and originality.

5.2 Creativity and Freedom

Freedom of thought and actions enjoyed by the student in the family had been determined by applying the Sarker's Freedom Test on 179 boys and 193 girls of class VIII and IX. The present study revealed that freedom of thought and actions was an important aspect of family environment in relation to the creativity development. Graphical representations, correlation techniques, inferential statistics with gender difference and regression analysis had been applied to determine the relationship, to test the hypotheses and thereby to attain the objectives of the study. Regarding this aspect of family environment, six hypotheses were considered in this study. Besides these, Freedom of students was considered as a predictor of Total Fluency, Total Flexibility and Total Originality in regression analysis included in the last three hypotheses.

Hypothesis – H_4:

There would be significant difference between Freedom and Restriction group boys in Fluency, Flexibility and Originality scores of verbal and non-verbal creativity.

This hypothesis was totally accepted in this present study. That meant, there was a significant difference between 'Freedom' and 'Restriction' groups of boys in Fluency, Flexibility and Originality scores of both verbal and non-verbal creativity. Obviously, it was found that the 'Freedom group' of boys was always superior to the 'Restriction group' in mean scores of Fluency, Flexibility as well as in Originality of both verbal and non-verbal creativity (Section 4.6.2.1).

Graphical representations in the Figures 4.5.1.1 and 4.5.1.2 (For verbal and non-verbal Fluency), 4.5.2.1 and 4.5.2.2 (For verbal and non-verbal Flexibility), 4.5.3.1 and 4.5.3.2 (For verbal and non-verbal Originality) showed that mean scores of the components of creativity more or less gradually increased with the increase of Freedom score for boys group. These graphical representations also indicated the interpretation.

Hypothesis – H_5:

There would be significant difference between Freedom and Restriction group girls in Fluency, Flexibility and Originality scores of verbal creativity.

The hypothesis – H_5 might be accepted in the study. The study revealed that the 'Freedom group' girls was advanced to the 'Restriction group' girls in Fluency, Flexibility and Originality components of verbal creativity. Hence, the differences between the two groups in mean scores of Fluency and Originality were significant but the difference between them in mean scores of Flexibility (V. C.) was not significant at 0.05 level of significance (significant at $p = 0.059$, little differed from $p = 0.05$) [Section 4.6.2.2.1].

Graphical Representation in the Figures 4.5.1.1 (For verbal Fluency), 4.5.2.1 (For verbal Flexibility) and 4.5.3.1 (For verbal Originality) indicated that mean scores of Fluency, Flexibility and Originality of verbal creativity for girls group increased haphazardly with the increase of Freedom score and thereby supported the interpretation.

Hypothesis – H_6:

There would be significant difference between Freedom and Restriction group girls in Fluency, Flexibility and Originality scores of non-verbal creativity.

The present study revealed that the above hypothesis was totally rejected. That meant, there was no significant difference between 'Freedom' group and 'Restriction' group in Fluency, Flexibility and Originality of non-verbal creativity (Section 4.6.2.2.2)

Graphical Representations in the Figures 4.5.1.2 (For non-verbal Fluency), 4.5.2.2 (For non-verbal Flexibility) and 4.5.3.2 (For non-verbal Originality) showed that for the girls group, the mean scores of the components of non-verbal creativity were changing non-uniformly with the increase of Freedom score. These figures supported the said interpretation.

Hypothesis – H_9:

There would be significant relationship between Freedom of students and components of verbal creativity (Fluency, Flexibility, Originality) of both verbal and non-verbal creativity tests for boys.

Pearson's Correlation Technique had been applied to find out the relationship between the Freedom score and the scores of Creativity components. The present study showed that there were positive significant relationships existed between Freedom and components of both verbal and non-verbal creativity (except non-verbal originality). Thus, the hypothesis - H_9 was accepted in this study (Section 4.7.1.1).

Hypothesis - H_{10}:

There would be significant relationship between Freedom of students and components of verbal creativity (Fluency, Flexibility, Originality) for girls.

The study revealed that the Freedom of the girls in the families was significantly correlated with Fluency and Originality components of verbal creativity but insignificantly correlated with Flexibility component ($p = 0.053$, slightly differed from $p = 0.05$). Thus, the above hypothesis was mostly accepted in this study. (Section 4.7.1.2.1).

Hypothesis - H_{11}:

There would be significant relationship between Freedom of students and components of non-verbal creativity (Fluency, Flexibility, Originality) for girls.

In the present study, it was found that the Freedom of girl students was not significantly correlated with Fluency, Flexibility and Originality of non-verbal creativity. In other words, there was no significant relationship between Freedom of girl students and the components of non-verbal creativity. Hence, the hypothesis was totally rejected in the study.

Hypothesis - H_{15}:

Freedom of students, Socio-economic status would be significant predictors of Total Fluency.

The present study revealed that Freedom was the first variable entered in the step-wise multiple regression analysis. Freedom was the relatively greater contributing factor (95%) in Total Fluency of creativity with respect to the other predictor variables - Socio-economic Status and Family Tension (Fig. 4.8.1).

Hypothesis - H_{16}:

Freedom of students, Socio-economic Status would be significant predictors of Total Flexibility.

It was found in the present study that Freedom of students was the first predictor variable entered in the regression analysis. Here, also, Freedom of students had the greater contribution (92%) among the three predictor variables (Fig. 4.8.2).

Hypothesis - H_{17}:

Freedom of students, Socio-economic Status would be significant predictors of Total Originality.

It was found in the present study that Freedom variable entered in the second step of multiple regression analysis. Here, Freedom had the highest contributing factor (89%) to the Total Originality of Creativity.

Findings:

Regarding the variable 'Freedom', the obtained findings were as follows:

- For boys 'Freedom group' was always significantly superior to the 'Restriction group' in Fluency, Flexibility and Originality of both verbal and non-verbal creativity.
- For girls 'Freedom group' was significantly advanced to the 'Restriction group' in Fluency and Originality and merely advanced in Flexibility component of verbal creativity.
- For girls 'Freedom group' was not significantly differed from the 'Restriction group' in Fluency, Flexibility and Originality components of non-verbal creativity.
- For boys, there were positive significant relationships existed between Freedom and components of both verbal and non-verbal creativity.

- For girls, there were positive significant relationships existed between Freedom and Fluency and Originality (insignificant for Flexibility) components of Verbal creativity.
- Freedom of students was a great contributing predictor variable to Total Fluency among the two variables.
- Freedom of students was also a greater contributing predictor variable to Total Flexibility of creativity.
- Freedom of students was the greater contributing predictor variable to Total Originality among the two variables.

Discussion

Freedom of thought and actions enjoyed by the students in their families was considered as an important variable in the present study. Objectives of the present study were to determine, whether there was any relationship between Freedom and Creativity with its different components – Fluency, Flexibility, Originality. The present study revealed that Freedom was positive significantly correlated with creativity along with its three components – Fluency, Flexibility and Originality. For boys, 'Freedom group' was always significantly superior to the 'Restriction group' in both verbal and non-verbal creativity. Also, for girls, 'Freedom group' was significantly advanced to the 'Restriction group', in verbal creativity. These findings indicated that the students who had got more freedom in thinking, in playing with different items in making models, games, in expressing ideas in their families had developed their creativity. These findings were in tune with the theoretical expectation. But in case of non-verbal creativity, the 'Freedom group' girls was not significantly differed from the 'Restriction group' girls. Also, for girls, the components of non-verbal creativity were not significantly correlated with freedom. These findings might get support from the views that by nature girls were verbally developed and free environment encouraged them to be more advanced but for non-verbal activities, not only freedom made them superior to the others, they needed extra ones in the development of creative potential in this society.

But in each the three Regression Equation Y (Total Fluency or Total Flexibility or Total Originality) contained a high value constant. It indicated when all the X (Freedom, Socio-economic Status) were zero, Y had that constant value. It implied that creativity was a multifaceted phenomenon and its development depended on so many factors.

The following statements supported the above findings:

i) Tibetan spiritual leader the 14th Dalai Lama (17th March, 2010), stressed the need for individual freedom to ensure overall growth of human creativity in His address on "Human Rights Through Universal Responsibility" at the Assembly auditorium of Madhya Pradesh, India. According to him, "Without freedom, one's creativity cannot bloom. Right to freedom is pivotal for the progress of any society".

ii) The problem of free will and the problem of creativity are, in some respects, one and the same. They can both be solved together (Philip N. Jhnson-Laird).

iii) Creativity encourages and demands complete freedom to accept and express the varied responses. A positive environment or situation that is open democratic and free may be said to contribute positively to the development of creative potential. On the other hand, a closed society, culture or situation may act as a strong deterrent to the development of initiative within the individual (Richa Sharma, 2011).

iv) True freedom is to be like the wind - coming with nothing and leaving with nothing. It is to allow all that has gone into anything we create to fully dissolve and dissipate back into its fundamental components so they can be available for the next creation.

v) Eric Barker (3rd August, 2011) mentioned his view in a new way. According to him, 'A curvilinear effect of constraint on creativity was identified such that a moderate degree of constraint was more conducive to creativity than either a high or a low degree. While some amount of choice is important for encouraging creativity, too much can be counterproductive, which runs counter to many popular theories of creativity.

vi) "Paradoxically, creativity thrives on the tension between freedom and constraint", says Brent Rosso (2011), an organizational psychology Professor at Montana State University who studies the balance between freedom and constraint in the product development process. "They are the yin and yang of creativity".

5.3 Creativity and Socio-economic Status

Socio-economic Status (SES) of the families of the students considered as the sample of the present study had been determined by applying the Sarker's Socio-economic Status Test on 179 boys and 193 girls of class VIII and IX. For family environment, Socio-economic Status was an important aspect in relation to the creativity development of the student. Graphical representations, correlation techniques, inferential statistics with gender difference and regression analysis had been applied to determine the relationship, to test the hypotheses and thereby to attain the objectives of the study. Regarding this aspect of family environment, five hypotheses were considered in this study. Besides these, Socio-economic Status was considered as a predictor of Total Fluency, Total Flexibility and Total Originality in regression analysis mentioned in the last three hypotheses.

Hypothesis – H_7:

There would be significant difference between High and Low Socio-economic Status group boys in Fluency, Flexibility and Originality scores of verbal and non-verbal creativity.

This hypothesis was rejected in the present study. There was no significant difference between High group SES boys and Low group SES boys in Fluency, Flexibility and Originality of both verbal and non-verbal creativity (except non-verbal Originality) [Section 4.6.3.1].

Graphical Representation in the Figures 4.5.4.1 and 4.5.4.2 (For verbal and non-verbal Fluency), 4.5.5.1 and 4.5.5.2 (For verbal and non-verbal Flexibility), 4.5.6.1 and 4.5.6.2 (For verbal and non-verbal Originality) showed that means scores of the components of creativity increased and suddenly fell down from the peak at higher score of Socio-economic Status. It indicated that there was no uniform relationship between the components of creativity and Socio-economic status of the families.

Hypothesis - H_8:

There would be significant difference between High and Low Socio-economic Status group girls in Fluency, Flexibility and Originality scores of verbal and non-verbal creativity.

The hypothesis H_8 was accepted in the present study. The study revealed that the High group SES girls was significantly superior to the Low group SES girls in Fluency, Flexibility and Originality of both verbal and non-verbal creativity (except in case of non-verbal Fluency) [Section 4.6.3.2].

Graphical Representation in the Figures 4.5.4.1 and 4.5.4.2 (For verbal and non-verbal Fluency), 4.5.5.1 and 4.5.5.2 (For verbal and non-verbal Flexibility), 4.5.6.1 and 4.5.6.2 (For verbal and non-verbal Originality) showed that mean scores of the components of both verbal and non-verbal creativity for girls group haphazardly increased with increase of Socio-economic Status. But the mean score of non-verbal fluency more or less existed at the same point (26.00) with the increase of Socio-economic Status. Thus, the graphs supported the above interpretations.

Hypothesis - H_{12}:

There would be significant relationship between socio-economic status and components of verbal creativity (Fluency, Flexibility, Originality) for boys.

This hypothesis was totally rejected in the present study. That meant, there was no significant relationship between Socio-economic Status and components of verbal creativity for boys (Section 4.7.2.1.1).

Hypothesis - H_{13}:

There would be significant relationship between Socio-economic Status and components of non-verbal creativity (Fluency, Flexibility, Originality) for boys.

The present study revealed that the Socio-economic Status of the boys' families was significantly correlated with Flexibility and Originality but not with Fluency (significant at $p = 0.056$ slightly differed from $p = 0.05$). Thus, the hypothesis was accepted in this study (Section - 4.7.2.1.2).

Hypothesis - H_{14}:

There would be significant relationship between Socio-economic Status and components of creativity (Fluency, Flexibility, Originality) of both verbal and non-verbal creativity tests for girls.

This hypothesis was accepted in this present study. This study showed that Socio-economic Status of the families of the girls was significantly correlated with Fluency. Flexibility and Originality components of both verbal and non-verbal creativity (Except non-verbal Fluency) [Section - 4.7.2.2].

Hypothesis - H_{15}:

Freedom of students, Socio-economic Status would be significant predictors of Total Fluency.

The present study revealed that Socio-economic Status was the second predictor variable entered in the step-wise multiple regression analysis. Socio-economic Status was the second highest (5%) contributing factor to Total Fluency of Creativity (Fig. 4.8.1).

Hypothesis - H_{16}:

Freedom of students, Socio-economic Status would be significant predictors of Total Flexibility.

It was found in the present study that Socio-economic Status was the second variable entered in the step-wise multiple regression analysis. Socio-economic Status had 8% contribution in Total Flexibility of creativity among the two predictor variables (Fig. 4.8.2).

Hypothesis - H_{17}:

Freedom of students, Socio-economic Status would be significant predictors of Total Originality.

The present study showed that Socio-economic Status was the first variable entered in the step-wise multiple regression analysis. Socio-economic Status had second contribution (11%) to Total Originality of Creativity among the three predictor variables (Fig. 4.8.3).

Findings

The following findings were found with respect to Socio-economic Status in the present study:

- For boys, there was no significant difference between High group SES and Low SES in Fluency, Flexibility and Originality of both verbal and non-verbal creativity.
- For girls, the High SES group was significantly superior to the Low SES group in Fluency, Flexibility and Originality of both verbal and non-verbal creativity.
- For boys, there was positive significant relationship between SES and components of non-verbal creativity.
- For girls, there was positive significant relationship between SES and components of both verbal and non-verbal creativity.

- Socio-economic Status (SES) was the second contributing factor to Total Fluency.
- Socio-economic Status (SES) was also the second contributing variable to Total Flexibility.
- Socio-economic Status was the second contributing variable to Total Originality among the two predictor variables.

Discussion

One of the objectives of the present study was to determine the relationship between creativity and Socio-economic Status of the families of the students considered as sample of the study. The study disclosed that there was a positive significant relationship existed between the components of verbal and non-verbal creativity and Socio-economic Status. But, there was no significant relationship existed between the components - Fluency, Flexibility and Originality and Socio-economic Status for boys group, in case of verbal creativity.

The present study also showed that for boys High Socio-economic Status group was not significantly differed from the Low Socio-economic Status group. It indicated that Socio-economic Status was not a factor in the development of creativity among the boys.

In the above findings, the argument was that exposure to outward world was similar for the boys of both High Socio-economic Status family and Low Socio-economic Status family in this society and culture. As a result, both High SES and Low SES boys were similar in the development of creativity. Thus, the difference between the two groups in Fluency, Flexibility, Originality of both verbal and non-verbal creativity was not significant. This finding was also in agreement with some research findings. Nichols (1964), Lichtenwalner and Maxwell (1969), Keenan and Victoria (1973), had got the findings that there was no significant difference in creativity between High and Low SES groups children.

Again, Mankar, Ugale, Rothe (2011) mentioned in their research findings that 'Socio-economic Status and Occupation of parents were showing insignificant correlation with the creativity of children. There was no impact of parent occupation on their children's creativity.

It was also found in the present study that girls of High Socio-economic Status families were significantly superior to the girls of Low Socio-economic Status families in Fluency, Flexibility and Originality of both verbal and non-verbal creativity. In this regard, it could be said that in the case of girls the nature of upbringing, was so much different for Low SES families and High SES families in this society as well as culture. The girls who come from High Socio-economic Status families perhaps have more freedom in order to express themselves, get more freedom to come out in the outer world, get more materials to play and, whereas the girls who come from Low Socio-economic Status families usually had to go through strict pressure and rules of this society. This finding got supports from many research-works.

The research works done by Ogletree and Ujlaki (1978), Niwas and Punia (2013), Saha (2012), Parsasirat, Foroughi *et al.* (2013), Rao and Satyapal (2011), got the findings as there were significant positive relationship between components of creativity and dimensions of Socio-economic Status.

It was also revealed in the present study that Socio-economic Status was an important contributing predictor variable in the three Regression Equations for Total Fluency, Total Flexibility and Total Originality. But, in each of the three Regression Equations, dependent variable Y (Total Fluency or Total Flexibility or Total Originality) contained a high value of constant. It indicated that when the predictor variables X (Freedom, Socio-economic Status) became zero, the Y had that constant value (interception of Y-axis). It implied that creativity and its components did not depend on the aspects of family environment only but also depended on the so many factors which were associated with the creativity development in the children.

5.4 Ideal Family Environment

In this section, the present researcher tried to establish an ideal family environment for the development of creativity in the children on the basis of findings and discussions regarding the aspects of family environment. This was the last objective of the present study. There were four aspects of family environment, namely; Freedom of thought and actions, Socio-economic Status had been considered in the present study.

Family environment refers to all sorts of moral and ethical values and emotional, social and intellectual climate set up by the family members to contribute to the wholesome development of an individual. Family with its physical, intellectual and emotional aspects shape a child's life in his journey towards self-fulfillment. A powerful home environment may be created for the child with the presentation of concepts such as; the encouragement of incidental learning, freedom to reactions of the environment, scopes of the physical materials, attention from adults and the close relationship between parents and the child.

Creativity is a complex and multi-faceted phenomenon. It has much areas and so many factors are associated to its development. In this study, a few of such factors are included in the family environment, but not all of them. For that reason, the researcher found out a high value of constant in the three Regression Equations for Total Fluency, Total Flexibility and Total Originality considering Freedom, Socio-economic Status as the predictor variables. However, in the present study, the following situations might be considered to create an ideal family environment for the development of creativity:

1) Freedom of Thought and Actions: The child should get complete freedom to accept and express the varied responses. Unrestricted, open and democratic situations are favourable to creativity development. The child should be encouraged to create games with spontaneity and provided materials and items, toys to make something or to play.

2) High Socio-economic Status: Socio-economic Status of the family should be high so far as possible. High economic condition is always helpful to provide materials and learning experiences to the child in the family. This is specially, essential for the girl students. This may be limited with the providing play-materials, equipment and physical components.

3) Low Family Tension and Stress: Family Tension is a negative factor for fostering creativity in the child. Minimum level of parental tension is favourable for creativity development. A healthy emotional climate may be created when the parents resolve the disagreements among them. But a moderate stressful setting may be favourable for creative productions. Sometimes, it makes the child to be more powerful, effective and challenged.

4) Establishment of Healthy Parental Bonds with Children: A good parental bond with children allows them autonomy, independence, psychological and emotional space. Parents can support to get the experience of tensions and stress that arise from challenging ideas and high expectations to live up to one's potential. They may help their child to cope with the strategies for stress.

6

SUMMARY AND CONCLUSION

This chapter contained the summary and conclusion of the study and some suggestions for the further research.

6.1 Summary

The summarized form of the present study is stated below:

Restatement of the Problem

The main purpose of this study was to find out the relationship between components of creativity and aspects of family environment (, *Socio-economic Status, Freedom of thought and actions*) of school going students in the Districts of Nadia and 24 Parganas (North) where various kind of people live. Thus, the problem was stated as: **Creativity in Relation to Socio-economic Status and Freedom in Family Environment.**

Objectives of the Study

The objectives of the present study were framed as follows:

1) To assess the verbal and non-verbal creativity of all the students in terms of fluency, flexibility and originality.

2) To study the gender difference in different components - fluency, flexibility and originality of both verbal and non-verbal creativity.

3) To study the difference between Freedom and Restriction group boys in fluency, flexibility and originality of both verbal and non-verbal creativity.

4) To study the difference between Freedom and Restriction group girls in fluency, flexibility and originality of both verbal and non-verbal creativity.

5) To study the difference between High and Low Socio-economic Status group boys in different components - fluency, flexibility and originality of both verbal and non-verbal creativity.

6) To study the difference between High and Low Socio-economic Status group girls in different components - fluency, flexibility and originality of both verbal and non-verbal creativity.

7) To study the relationship between Freedom of students and different components of both verbal and non-verbal creativity for boys.

8) To study the relationship between Freedom of students and different components of both verbal and non-verbal creativity for girls.

9) To study the relationship between Socio-economic Status and different components of both verbal and non-verbal creativity for boys.

10) To study the relationship between Socio-economic Status and different components of both verbal and non-verbal creativity for girls.

11) To develop a Multiple Regression Equation of Total Fluency on Freedom of students, Socio-economic Status.

12) To develop a Multiple Regression Equation of Total Flexibility on Freedom of students, Socio-economic Status.

13) To develop a Multiple Regression Equation of Total Originality on Freedom of students, Socio-economic Status.

14) To explain an ideal family environment for better development of creativity in children.

Hypotheses of the Study

Criterion of creativity is an independent measure of Fluency, Flexibility and Originality under both verbal test and non-verbal test.

Keeping in mind the objectives of the present study and findings of the review of related studies, the researcher formulated the following hypotheses:

H_1: There would be no significant difference between boys and girls in Fluency scores of verbal and non-verbal creativity.

H_2: There would be no significant difference between boys and girls in Flexibility scores of verbal and non-verbal creativity.

H_3: There would be no significant difference between boys and girls in Originality scores of verbal and non-verbal creativity.

H_4: There would be significant difference between Freedom and Restriction group boys in Fluency, Flexibility and Originality scores of verbal and non-verbal creativity.

H_5: There would be significant difference between Freedom and Restriction group girls in Fluency, Flexibility and Originality scores of verbal creativity.

H_6: There would be significant difference between Freedom and Restriction group girls in Fluency, Flexibility and Originality scores of non-verbal creativity.

H_7: There would be significant difference between High and Low Socio-economic Status group boys in Fluency, Flexibility and Originality scores of verbal and non-verbal creativity.

H_8: There would be significant difference between High and Low Socio-economic Status group girls in Fluency, Flexibility and Originality scores of verbal and non-verbal creativity.

H_9 : There would be significant relationship between Freedom of students and components of creativity (Fluency, Flexibility, Originality) of both verbal and non-verbal creativity tests for boys.

H_{10}: There would be significant relationship between Freedom of students and components of verbal creativity (Fluency, Flexibility, Originality) for girls.

H_{11} : There would be significant relationship between Freedom of students and components of non-verbal creativity (Fluency, Flexibility, Originality) of both verbal and non-verbal creativity tests for girls.

H_{12}: There would be significant relationship between Socio-economic Status and components of verbal creativity (Fluency, Flexibility, Originality) for boys.

H_{13}: There would be significant relationship between Socio-economic Status and components of non-verbal creativity (Fluency, Flexibility, Originality) for boys.

H_{14}: There would be significant relationship between Socio-economic Status and components of creativity (Fluency, Flexibility, Originality) of both verbal and non-verbal creativity tests for girls.

H_{15}: Freedom of students, Socio-economic Status would be significant predictors of Total Fluency.

H_{16}: Freedom of students, Socio-economic Status would be significant predictors of Total Flexibility.

H_{17}: Freedom of students, Socio-economic Status would be significant predictors of Total Originality.

Sample

The sample consisted of 372 school going students of class VIII and class IX from eight different types of schools of district Nadia and North 24 Parganas. All the selected schools were of Bengali Medium under West Bengal Board of Secondary Education. There were 179 boys and 193 girls in the sample. Different types of schools were selected randomly from the both districts- according to a particular ratio.

The intellectual development and functioning take a very sophisticated shape at Formal Operation Stage (Piaget,1952) as the child learns to deal with abstraction by logical thinking. Here the child, age of 11 and above, learns to utilize the tool of symbolism as effectively as possible in the process of thought and problem solving. He begins to construct relationships between concrete operations and between symbols. He also begins to look at problems in many ways and explore various solutions but in a very systematic and logical way. Keeping this aspect in mind, the investigator selected the students of class VIII and class IX as the sample for this study.

Variables

The main objectives of the study were: to identify the creative individuals, gender difference in components of creativity, relationships between components of creativity and two aspects of family environment. Thus, the variables for this study were as follows:

A) Independent Variables:

Independent variables in this study were as follows:

i) Freedom of thought and actions enjoyed by the students in the family,

ii) Socio-economic Status of the family,

iii) Gender.

B) Dependent Variables:

Dependent variables in this study were students' performance scores, only on three components of creativity, obtained from verbal and non-verbal creativity tests.

i) Fluency (verbal fluency, non-verbal creativity).

ii) Flexibility (verbal flexibility, non-verbal flexibility).

iii) Originality (verbal originality, non-verbal originality).

Methodology

The main purpose of the study was to determine the relationship between criterion (Creativity) and predictor variables (Freedom, Socio-economic Status). For this purpose, the descriptive survey method of educational research had been followed. In this study the researcher performed the investigation on pupils of secondary level (grade VIII and IX). Collected data were arranged according to their code numbers. The magnitude of the relationship was determined through the use of the coefficient of correlation with the help of computer software SPSS version 12.0. Besides this, graphical representation helped to describe the relationship clearly.

Inferential Statistics - analysis of variance (ANOVA), t-test had been applied to compare the ability between Boys and Girls, or between the groups - High and Low of each independent variable. The inferential statistics helps the researcher to test the hypotheses and to get some important inferences.

Multiple Regression analysis was done in this research to know to what extent creativity could be predicted on the basis of Freedom, Socio-economic Status.

Tools Used

The following tools were used to collect the data from the sample of the study:

1. Sarker's Creativity Test

a) Verbal Test of Creativity

- Game – 1 : Unusual Uses
- Game – 2 : Similarity Task
- Game – 3 : Consequences Tasks
- Game – 4 : Common Problem Tasks
- Game – 5 : Product Improvement Tasks

b) Non-verbal Test of Creativity

- Game – 1 : Circle Test
- Game – 2 : Incomplete Figures
- Game – 3(A) : Asking Questions
- Game – 3(B) : Asking Questions

2. Sarker's Freedom Test

3. Sarker's Socio-economic Status Test

6.2 Principal Findings of the Study

The principal findings of the present study were as follows:

Gender

- There was no significant difference between boys and girls in Fluency and Originality components of both verbal and non-verbal creativity.

- In flexibility component of creativity, there were significant differences existed between boys and girls. Girls were superior to boys in verbal Flexibility but boys were advanced to girls in non-verbal Flexibility.

Freedom

- For boys 'Freedom group' was always significantly superior to the 'Restriction group' in Fluency, Flexibility and Originality of both verbal and non-verbal creativity.
- For girls 'Freedom group' was significantly advanced to the 'Restriction group' in Fluency and Originality and merely advanced in Flexibility component of verbal creativity.
- For girls 'Freedom group' was not significantly differed from the 'Restriction group' in Fluency, Flexibility and Originality components of non-verbal creativity.
- For boys, there were positive significant relationships existed between Freedom and components of both verbal and non-verbal creativity.
- For girls, there were positive significant relationships existed between Freedom and Fluency and Originality (insignificant for Flexibility) components of Verbal creativity.
- Freedom of students was a great contributing predictor variable to Total Fluency among the three variables.
- Freedom of students was also a greater contributing predictor variable to Total Flexibility of creativity.
- Freedom of students was the greater contributing predictor variable to Total Originality among the three variables.

Socioeconomic Status:

- For boys, there was no significant difference between High group SES and Low SES in Fluency, Flexibility and Originality of both verbal and non-verbal creativity.

- For girls, the High SES group was significantly superior to the Low SES group in Fluency, Flexibility and Originality of both verbal and non-verbal creativity.
- For boys, there was positive significant relationship between SES and components of non-verbal creativity.
- For girls, there was positive significant between SES and components of both verbal and non-verbal creativity.
- Socio-economic Status (SES) was the second contributing factor to Total Fluency.
- Socio-economic Status (SES) was also the second contributing variable to Total Flexibility.
- Socio-economic Status was the second contributing variable to Total Originality among the three predictor variables.

6.3 Conclusion

Among the three types of environments - Family, School and Society; Family environment plays an important role in fostering creativity. Because, the child is born and brought up in the family and he is much more influenced by the parental attitude, care and supports, emotional climate and the degree of freedom of thought and actions at his developmental stage of life. Hence, the aspects of family environment should be highly correlated with the creativity and its different components - fluency, flexibility and originality according to the theoretical perspectives. On the basis of the findings and discussions of the study, the present researcher concluded the followings:

- Among the aspects of family environment under consideration, Freedom of thought and actions, Socio-economic Status are positively correlated with the components of both verbal and non-verbal creativity.

- Gender difference is not a contributing factor to the components of both verbal and non-verbal creativity. That is, the boys are not significantly superior to the girls in fluency, flexibility and originality scores of creativity. A healthy, stimulating family environment can promote the creative potential in the children irrespective of gender.

- Students who enjoy high freedom in thinking and actions in their families are more fluent, flexible and originator of new ideas and productions. Both the boys and the girls of 'Freedom group' are significantly advanced to the 'Restriction group' in fluency, flexibility and originality scores of creativity. But only in case of non-verbal creativity, freedom does not make any difference between the two groups of the girls.

- There is a positive significant relationship exists between Socio-economic Status and the components (Fluency, Flexibility, Originality) of both verbal and non-verbal creativity for girls groups. But, for the boys, High Socio-economic Status group is not significantly differed from the Low Socio-economic Status group in both verbal and non-verbal creativity. Boys of both High and Low Socio-economic Status families have the similar exposures to the outward world. Whereas the girls of High Socio-economic Status families enjoy more freedom and supportive environment than the girls of Low Socio-economic Status families in the society. Hence, the difference between the two groups (High and Low) Socio-economic Status families is significant for girls.

6.4 Educational Implications

Creativity is a mystery, and many people believe that it should remain mystery, because, too much scrutiny for knowing about it, may be dangerous, says an anxious Romantic. The cynical Realist assets a different proposition. Any research work is done for the shake of development of human beings and society. Research findings are used to establish some general directions, guidance and rules for development of creativity and not for suppressing this valuable potential of human beings. These are essentials because creativity potential always requires evocating, promoting and stimulating environments for its development in the children. Again, without development of this potential, it cannot be expressed properly. On the other hand, the area of creativity is large and versatile and so many factors are associated with it. In these regards, every research on creativity development is important and significant to the society. The findings of this research also had potential educational implications like other studies. The present study re-affirmed the development of creative potential of school-going children in their families and also the importance of family environment in nurturing the creativity.

The present study highlighted the relationships among the different aspects of family environment and the components of creativity. It was found that there was no significant difference existed between boys and girls in their creativity development. In other words, the development was not greater in either boys or girls. This finding indicated that all the children, irrespective of their gender, were capable to develop their creative potential subject to suitable supportive environment. It suggested that the family should take care in nurturing creativity in their children without considering their gender.

One of the major implications of the study was that it provided the evidences that the components of creativity was significantly correlated with Freedom of children. This indicated that the students who had more freedom of thought and actions in their families, got better scopes for creativity development, as results better scores in creativity tests. This implies that the open, free, democratic family environment where the child enjoyed freedom in thinking and actions, was always conducive for creativity development. But the study found out the different results for girls in non-verbal creativity. This finding also demanded that only freedom was not a sufficient condition for girls in non-verbal performances.

The present study also revealed that Socio-economic Status of the family had influence on creativity. This was true only for girl students. Because, in this society and culture, girls of High and Low Socio-economic Status families did not get similar scopes in freedom of thought and actions and in exposure to outward world. Whereas the boys of both High and Low Socio-economic Status families got similar scopes in that field areas. Hence, there was no significant difference found out between the boys group of High and Low Socio-economic Status families in the components of both verbal and non-verbal creativity. These findings suggested that Socio-economic Status should be high especially for the families of girl students in providing freedom to play, to respond and to involve in various activities of daily life.

Regression analysis showed in the present study that though the aspects of family environment had contributions to Total Fluency, Total Flexibility and Total Originality, a high value of constant was found in each of the three regression equations. It indicated that creativity development did not depend only on these aspects of family environment but depended on other unknown so many factors.

BIBLIOGRAPHY

Aggarwal, J. C. (2004). *Essential of Educational Psychology*. New Delhi: Vikas Publishing House Pvt. Ltd.

Albert, R. S. (1978). Observation and suggestions regarding giftedness, familiar influence, and the achievement of eminence. *Gifted Child Quarterly, 28* 201– 211.

Amabile, T. M. & Gryskiewicz, N. D. (1989). The creative environment scales: Work environment inventory. *Creativity Research Journal, 2(4)* 231 – 253.

Amabile, T. M. (2003). *The social psychology of creativity*. New York: Springer-Verlag.

Anderson, H. H. (1959). *Creativity and Its Cultivation*. New York: Harper.

Anderson, H. H. (1961-62). *Creativity and Education*. Educational Horizons. Winter, 123 – 129.

Anderson, H. H. (Editor) (1965). *Creativity in childhood and adolescence: A variety of approaches*. Palc. Alto, California: Science and Behaviour Books.

Arieti, S. (1976). *Creativity: The magic synthesis*. New York: Basic Books.

Arora, G. L. (1978). Relationship of Sex with Creativity, General Anxiety, Vocational Anxiety and Teaching Success. *J. of Edu. and Psychol., 36(3)* 133 – 139.

Baer, J. (2003). Sex differences. In *Creativity Research Handbook*, ed. M. A. Runco. Cresskill, N. J.: Hampton Press, 3.

Barker, E. (Aug., 2011). Does creativity require freedom or constraints? *Business Insider*.

Barron, F. & Harrington, D. (1981). Creativity, intelligence and personality. *Annual Review of Psychology, 32* 439 – 476.

Barron, F. (1958). The Psychology of Creativity. *In Encyclopaedia Britannica,* New York: 711 - 712.

Barron, F. (1969). *The Creative Person and the Creative Process.* New York: Holt.

Baruch, D. (1937). A study of reported tension in interparental relationships, as coexistent with behaviour adjustment in young children. *Journal of Experimental Education.*

Basantia, J. M. (2002). *A Critical Study on the Impact of Socio-economic Status, Home and School Environment and Some Psycho-social Constraints on the Academic Achievement of Students belonging to some isolated Tribal groups of Orissa.* Ph. D. Thesis (unpublished), Kalyani; University of Kalyani.

Berk, L. E. (2002). Make-Believe Play: Wellspring for Development of Self-Regulation. In *Play = Learning: How play motivates and enhances children's cognitive and social emotional growth.* Singer, D. G. *et al.* (Eds.). N. Y. : Oxford Univ. 74 - 100.

Bharadwaj, R. (1980). Intelligence, sex and age as correlates of the components of creativity. *Asian Journal of Psychology and Education, 16(3)* 41 - 44.

Bhogayata, C. K. (1986). *A Study of the Relationship among Creativity, Self-Concept and Locus of Control,* Ph. D. Edu. Thesis, Sagar University.

Biswas, P. C. (1988). *Reactions to Frustration in School Children.* Ph. D. Thesis (unpublished), Kalyani: University of Kalyani.

Blommers, P. & Lindquist, E. F. (1965). *Elementary Statistical Methods in Psychology and Education.* London: University of London Press Ltd.

Blood, R. O. (1958). The effect of the wife's employment on family power structure. *Social Forces.*

Bloom, B. (1985). *Developing talent in young people.* New York: Ballantine.

Bradley, R. H. & Corwyn, R. F. (2002). Socioeconomic Status and Child Development. *Annual Review of Psychology, 53* 371-399. Retrieved August 3, 2014, from www.arjournals.annualreviews.org

Brent, D. & Rosso, B. D. (2011). *Creativity and Constraints: Exploring the Role of Constraints in the Creative Processes of Research and Development Teams.* USA. Montana State University.

Bruner, J. S. (1962). The Conditions of Creativity. In H. E. Gruber, G. Terrell and M. Wertheimer (Ed.), *Contemporary Approaches to Creative Thinking,* N. Y.: Atherton Press.

Chapin, F. S. (1928). A quantitative scale for rating the home and social environment of middle-class families in an urban environment, a first approximation to the measurement of socio-economic status. *Journal of Educational Psychology.*

Chapin, F. S. (1942). A revision of Chapin's Social Status Scale. *American Sociological Review, 7* 362–369.

Chaudhary, G. G. (1983). *An Investigation into the Trends of Creative Thinking Ability of Pupils of Age Group 11+ to 13+ in Relation to Some Psychological correlates.* Unpublished Ph. D. Thesis, Sardar Patel University.

Cohen, L. M. (1989). A continuum of adaptive creative behaviours. *Creativity Research Journal, 2* 169 – 183.

Coone, J. A. (1969). *Cross-Cultural Study of Sex Differences in Development of Creative Thinking Abilities.* Dissertation Abstracts *29(12-13)* 4828 – 2829.

Dalbec, S. E. (1966). *Creative Development over a Three-Year Period in a Catholic Liberal Arts College.* Master's Research Paper, University of Minnesota.

Das, N. G. (2003). *Statistical Methods in Commerce, Accountancy and Economics* (Part – 1), Calcutta: M. Das & Co.

De Bono, E. (1993). *Serious creativity: using the power of lateral thinking to create new ideas.* New York: Harper Business

Deshmukh, M. N. (1977). *Creativity in class rooms.* New Delhi: Vikash Publishing House Pvt. Ltd.

Dharmangagadan, B. (1981). *Creativity in School Children – An Analytical Study.* Ph. D. Thesis (Unpublished), Kerala Univ.

Drevdahl, J. E. (1956). *Some Developmental and Environmental Factors in Creativity.* Ed. C. W. Taylor. Widening Horizons in Creativity, New York: Wiley.

Dreyer, A. S. & Wells, M. B. (Feb.,1966). Parental Values, Parental Control, and Creativity in Young Children. *Journal of Marriage and Family,28(1)* 83-88. Retrieved August 14, 2014, from http://www.jstor.org/stable/350047

Dudek, S. Z. & Hall, W. (1991). Personality consistency: eminent architects 25 years later. *Creativity Research Journal, 4* 213 – 232.

Dudek, S. Z. (2003). Art and Aesthetics. In *Creativity Research Handbook*, ed. M. A. Runco. Cresskill, N. J.: Hampton Press, 2.

Dudek, S. Z. *et al.* (1993). Cumulative and proximal influences of the social environment on creative potential. *J. Genet. Psychol., 154* 487 – 499.

Ebel, R. L., Rogers, M. B. & Victor, H. N. (Ed.). (1969). *Encyclopaedia of Educational Research*, 4th Edition, Collier, London: Macmillan.

Edwards, B. (2012). *Drawing on the Right Side of the Brain.* Los Angeles: Tarcher.

Ellermeyer, D. (1993). Enhancing creativity through play: a discussion of parental and environmental factors. In *Early Childhood and Creativity: a Scoping Exercise-Key Studies.*

Erickson, M. C. (1946). Child rearing and social status. *Amer. J. Sociol., 52* 190–192.

Faizi, M. *et al.* (2013). *Design Guidelines of Residential Environments to Stimulate Children's Creativity.* Tehran: Shahid Rajaee Teacher Training University, 16788 – 15811.

Fallding, H. (1968). The family and the idea of a cardinal role. Handel, G. (Ed.). *The Psychological Interior of the Family.* London: George Allen & Unwin.

Feist, G. J. & Runco, M. A. (1993). Trends in the creativity literature: an analysis of research in the *Journal of Creative Behaviour*, Creativity *Research Journal, 6* 271 – 286.

Feldman, D. H. (1994). *Creativity: Dreams, insights and transformations.* In D. H. Felman, M.

Ferguson, G. A. (1985). *Statistical Analysis in Psychology and Education.* Singapore: McGraw-Hill International Book Company. 5th Ed.

Fliegler, L. (1961). *Dimensions of Creative Process.* Michael Andrews (Ed.), Creativity and Psychological Health. New York: Syracuse University Press, 14.

Franklin, B. S. and Richards, P. N. (1977). Effects on children's divergent thinking abilities of a period of direct teaching for divergent production. *British Journal of Educational Psychology, 47* 66–70.

Gagneja, S. C. (1972). *A Study of Creativity in Ninth Class Students in Relation to Sex, Residential Background, Academic Achievement and Parental Occupation*. Master's Dissertation, Punjab Univ.

Galton, F. (1869). *Hereditary, Genius*, London: Macmillan.

Gardner, H. (1994). *Creative Minds*. New York, Basic Books.

Garnett, A. C. (1960), Freedom and Creativity. In *Proceedings and Address of the American Philosophical Association, 34* 25 – 39.

Garrett, H. E. (1962). *Statistics in Psychology and Education*, Bombay: Allied Pacific Pvt. Ltd.

Gaynor, J. L. R. & Runco, M. A. (1992). Family size, birth order, age-interval and the creativity of children. *Journal of Creative Behaviour, 26* 108 – 118.

Getzels, J. W. (1964). *Creative thinking, Problem solving, and Instruction. In E. R. Hilgard (Ed.): Theories of Learning and Instruction*. Chicago, University of Chicago Press, 240 – 267.

Goel, S. P. (2004). Effect of gender, home and environment on educational aspirations. *Journal of Community Guidance and Research, 21(1)* 77 – 81.

Gordon, W. J. (1961). *Synectics*. New York: Harper and Brothers.

Gowan, J. C. (1972). *Development of the Creative Individual*. San Diego: Robert Kna

Goyal, R. P. (1973). Creativity and School Climate: An exploratory study. *Journal of Psychological Researches, 17(2)* 77 – 80.

Guilford J. P. (1959). Traits of Creativity. In *Anderson Harold H. (Ed.), Creativity and Its Cultivation*. New York: Harper and Row, 142 – 161.

Guilford, J. P. (1950). Creativity. *American Psychologist, 5(9)* 444 – 454.

Guilford, J. P. (1962). Creativity: Its measurement and development: In *Parnes, S. J. and Harding H. F. A Source Book for Creative Thinking*. New York: Charles Scribners Sons, 151–158.

Guilford, J. P. (1962). Potentiality for Creativity. *Gifted Child Quarterly, 6* 87–90.

Guilford, J. P. (1964). *Progress in Discovery of Intellectual Factors*. In C. W. Taylor's (Ed.), Widening Horizons of Creativity, N. Y. Wiley.

Guilford, J. P. (1967). Creativity: Yesterday, Today and Tomorrow. *Journal of Creative Behaviour, 1(1)* 3–13.

Guilford, J. P. (1970). Creativity: Retrospect and Prospect. *Journal of Creative Behaviour, 4* 149–168.

Gupta, P. K. (2004). Education for Creativity: A Global Issue. *NEHU Journal of Social Science and Humanities*, North Eastern Hill University Publication, *2(1)* 27–30.

Gupta, P. K. (2006). *Education for Creativity: Training, Research and Implications*, New Delhi: Cosmo Publications.

Halpin, W. G., Payne, D. A. & Ellett, J. (1973). Use of a factored biographical inventory to identify differentially gifted adolescents. *Psychol. Rep. 35* 1195 – 1204.

Hargreaves, D. J. (1977). Sex Roles in Divergent Thinking. *British Journal of Edu. Psychol., 47* 125–132.

Harrington, D. M. *et al.* (1983). Predicting creativity in preadolescence from divergent thinking in early childhood. *Journal Personal Soc. Psychol., 45* 609 – 623.

Hasirci, D. & Demirkan, H. (2003). Creativity in Learning Environments: the case of two sixth grade art rooms. *J. Creat. Behav. 37* 17 – 41.

Helson, R. (1990). Creativity in women: inner and outer views over time. Theories of Creativity, eds. M. A. Runco. R. S. Albert, Newbury Park, CA: Sage, 46 – 58.

Henry, A. F. (1956). Family role structure and self-blame. *Social Forces.*

Herbst, P. G. (1952). The measurement of family relationships. *Human Relationship, 5(1)* 3–30.

Hetherington, E. M. & Deur, J. L. (March, 1971). The Effects of Father Absence on Child Development. *Young Children,26(4)* 233-242, 244, 246, 248. Retrieved August 16, 2014, from http://www.jstor.org/stable/42643357

Hoffman, L. W. (1960). Effects of the employment of mothers on parental power relations and the division of household tasks. *Marriage & Family Living.*

Hurlock, E. B. (1974). *Personality Development.* New Delhi: Tata McGraw Hill.

Hussain, M. G. (1974). Creativity and Sex Difference. *Psychol. Studies, 19* 127–129.

Jacobs, T. (18 June, 2013). Dim Lighting Sparks Creativity. *Pacific Standard: The Science of Society.*

Jain, R. (1975). Originality, Intelligence and Interest in Scientific Pursuits as Correlates of Teaching Proficiency. *Indian Psychol. Review, 14(2),* 44 – 47.

Jinzhen, W. *et al.* (2004). Association of diet and lifestyle with blood pressure in the Guangxi Hei Yi Zhuang and Han populations. *Public Health Nutrition* 12 553 – 561.

John, C. D. (1988). *Familial and School Correlates of Creativity – A Study of Standard IX Students.* M. Phil. Thesis, Dept. of Education, Bangalore University.

Kaul, L. (1984). *Methodology of Educational Research.* New Delhi: Vikas Publishing House Pvt. Ltd.

Keenan, J. F. & Victoria, J. (Spring, 1973). The Relationship of Certain Socio-cultural and Community Factors among Sixth grade Students to Creativity in Art. *Review of Research in Visual and Environmental Education, 1(1)* 42-54. Retrieved August 2, 2014, from http://www.jstor.org/stable/20715145

Kim, K. H. (2011). The creativity crisis: The decrease in creative thinking scores on the Torrance Tests of Creative Thinking. *Creativity Research Journal, 23* 285–295.

Kneller, G. F. (1965). *The Act and Science of Creativity,* New York: Holt.

Kuppuswamy, B. (1962). *Manual of Social-economic Status Scale (Urban),* Delhi: Manasayan.

Lama, D. (2010). *Freedom Must for Human Creativity.* www.dalailama.com

Lewin, K. (1946). Behavior and Development as a function of the social situation. Charmichael, L. (Ed.). *Manual of Child Psychology.* New York: Wiley.

Lichtenwalner, J. S. & Maxwell, J. W. (Dec., 1969). The Relationship of Birth Order and Socio-Economic Status to the Creativity of Preschool Children. *Child Development, 40(4)* 1241–1247. Retrieved August 2, 2014, from http://www.jstor.org/stable/1127028

Ligon, E. M. (1957). *The Psychology of Christian Personality.* New York: MacMillan.

Mackinnon, D. W. (1966). Instructional media in the nurturing of creativity. C.W. Taylor and Frank E. Williams (Ed). *Instructional Media and Creativity.* New York: John Wiley and Sons, Inc., 179 – 216.

Mangal, S. K. (2005). *Advanced Educational Psychology.* New Delhi: Prentice-Hall of India Pvt. Ltd., *2nd Ed.*

Mankar, J. P., Ugale, S. U. & Rothe, S. P. (2011). Creativity in children as function of parent occupation and socio-economic status. *International Multidisciplinary Research Journal, 1(4)* 17–18. Retrieved August 3, 2014, from http://irjs.info_index

Mari, S. (1971). *Creativity of American and Arab Rural Youth: A Cross-Cultural Study.* Dissertation Abstracts International *31(12-A)* 6407–6408.

Mednick, S. A. (1962). The associative basis for the creative process. *Psychology Review, 69* 200 – 232.

Mehdi, B. (1971). *Manual: Verbal test of creative thinking.* Aligarh.

Mehdi, B. (Editor) (1977). *Creativity in Teaching and Learning.* Report of the Workshop conducted at the Regional College of Education, Mysore from 27th Jan. to 1st February, 1975, RCE (NCERT), Mysore, 20 - 23.

Miller, B. C. & Gerard, D. (July,1979). Family Influences on the Development of Creativity in Children: An Integrative Review. *The Family Coordinator, 28(3)* 295–312.Retrieved August 7, 2014, from http://www.jstor.org/stable/581942

Minuchin, S. (1974). *Family and Family Therapy.* London: Tavistock Publications.

Mitra, R. (1975). *Some determinants of academic performance in preadolescent children.* Ph. D. Thesis (unpublished). Calcutta University.

Mukherjee, M. (2007). *A study of creativity in relation to need-achievement, manifest anxiety and level of aspiration.* Ph. D. Thesis (unpublished), Kalyani: University of Kalyani.

Mumford, M. D. & Gustafson, S. B. (1988). Creativity Syndrome: Integration, Application and Innovation. *Psychological Bulletin 103* 27 – 43.

Murphy, G. (1947). *Personality.* New York: Harper and Row, 453.

Murray, B. (Nov., 2002). A ticking clock means a creativity drop: Time pressure quashes creativity because it limits people's freedom to ponder different options and directions. *American Psychological Association, 33(10)* 24.

Musick, K. (Oct., 2012). *"Are both parents better than one?"*. Retrieved August 6, 2014, from http://www.papers.ccpr.ucla.edu

Myers, R. E. and Torrance, E. T. (1964). *Invitation to thinking and doing,* Boston: Genn and Co.

Neelam, S. (2008). *Hindi ke Evam Marathi Aur Bangla Ke Hindi main Anudit Upanayason mein Vyakt Samajik Sarokar.* Jammu: University of Jammu.

Nichols, R. C. (Dec.,1964). Parental Attitudes of Mothers of Intelligent Adolescents and Creativity of Their Children. *Child Development, 35(4)* 1041–1049. Retrieved August 7, 2014, from http://www.jstor.org/stable/1126851

Nijhawan, H. K. (1972). *Anxiety in School Children.* New Delhi: Wiley Eastern Pvt. Ltd.

Niwas, R. & Punia, V. (May, 2013). The Relationship between Socio-Economic Status and Scientific Creativity of Scheduled Caste Students. *Indian Journal of Applied Research, 3(5)* 169–172. Retrieved August 7, 2014, from www.theglobaljournals.com_ijar_ file.php_val=May_2013_1367501631_b5612_51

Norah, Al-sulaiman (2009). *Cross-cultural Studies and Creative Thinking Abilities.* Saudi Arabia: King Saud University.

Ochse, R. (1993). *Before the gates of excellence: The determinants of creative genius.* Cambridge, England: Cambridge University Press.

Ogburn, W. F., & Nimkoff, M. F. (1972). *A Handbook of Sociology.* New Delhi: Eurasia Publishing House.

Ogletree, E. J. & Ujlaki, W. (Dec.,1973). Effects of Social Class Status on Tests of Creative Behavior. *The Journal of Educational Research,67(4)* 149-152. Retrieved August 7, 2014, from http://www.jstor.org/stable/27536552

Olszewski, P., Kulieke, M. J. & Buescher, T. (1987). The influence of the family environment on the development of talent: A literature review, *Journal for the Education of the Gifted, 11* 6 – 28.

Olszewski-Kubilius, P. (2001). The social and emotional development of gifted children: What do we know? *Parenting practices that promote talent development, creativity and optimal adjustment*. Prufrock Press, 205 - 212.

Panda, D. N. (1997). Impact of creativity and adjustment on academic achievement. *The Education Review, 1(2).*

Pande, A. & Nanda, P. (2005). Quality of nursery school education and school readiness of children. *Research Abstract-in International Conference of GATS and Education,* Department of Education and Community Service, Patiala: Punjabi University.

Pandey, R. C. (1980). *A Study of Creativity as related to Rural-Urban Background, Sex, Socio-economic Status and Formal Education, (with special reference to the High School Students of Kumaun Division)*. Ph. D. Thesis, Kumaun University.

Paramesh, C. R. (1969). Creativity and Intelligence on temperament. *Journal of Education and Psychology, 34(3)* 159 - 161.

Pareek, S. S. (1966). *An Investigation into Creative Thinking of the Students at Different Age Levels and the Relationship Between Creative Thinking and Other Related Factors.* Unpublished Master's Thesis, University of Rajasthan.

Pareek, U. & Trivedi, G. (1964). *Manual of Socio-economic Status Scale.* Delhi: Manasayan.

Parnes, S. J. & Brunelle, E. A. (1967). *The literature of creativity – Part–I, Journal of Creative Behaviour, 1(1)* 52 – 109.

Parnes, S. J. & Harding, H. F. (Eds.) (1962). *A Source Book for Creative Thinking.* New York: Charles Scribner's Sons.

Parnes, S. J. (1963, 1967). *Education and Creativity.* In J. C. Gowan, G. D. Domos and E. P. Torrance. *Creativity. Its Educational Implications,* New York: John Wiley and Sons, 33.

Parsasirat, Z. *et al.* (2013). Effect of Socioeconomic Status on Emersion Adolescent Creativity. *Asian Social Science, 9(4).*

Passi, B. K. (1972). Definition of Creativity – A review study. *Creativity Newsletter, 2(2)* 5 – 10.

Philip, N. & Johnson, L. (1988). Freedom and constraint in creativity. *The nature of creativity: contemporary psychological perspectives,* R. J. Sternberg (Ed.), Cambridge Univ. Press, 202 – 221.

Piaget, J. (1952). *The Origins of Intelligence in Children*, New York: International University Press.

Piirto, J. (1992). *Understanding those who create.* Dayton: Ohio Psychology Press.

Prakash, A. O. (1966). *Understanding of the Fourth Grade Scholars. A Study of the Creative Thinking of Indian Students.* Unpublished Master's Thesis, University of Minnesota.

Raina, M. K. & Chaturvedi, S. (1969). Effects of training in creative problem solving on fluency of thinking. *Indian Journal of Applied Psychology, 7* 71– 74.

Raina, M. K. (1971(a). Research developments in creativity in India. *Journal of Research and Development in Education, 3* 118 – 128.

Raina, M. K. (1971). Verbal and Non-verbal Creative Thinking Ability, A Study in Sex Difference, *J. of Edu. and Psychol., 29(3)* 175–179.

Raina, M. K. (Editor) (1980). *Creativity Research: International Perspective.* New Delhi, NCERT.

Rao, T. V. G. & Satyapal (2011). Socio-economic Status, Scheduled Caste and Creativity. *International Journal of Transformations in Business Management,*1(4), Retrieved August 6,2014, from http:// www.ijtbm.com

Rawat, M. S. & Agarwal, S. (1977). A Study of Creativity Thinking with reference to intelligence, age, sex, communities and income group. *Indian Psychological Review, 14(2)* 36 – 40.

Reis, S. M. (1999). Women and Creativity. *Encyclopaedia of Creativity.* San Diego. CA: Academic, 699 – 708.

Renjulli, J. S. (1973). *New Directions in Creativity,* Harper and Row.

Rhodes, C. (1997). Growth from deficiency creativity to being creativity. In M. A. Runco and R. Richards (Eds.), *Eminent creativity, everyday creativity and health.* Greenwich, C T: Ablex. 247 – 264.

Rose, L. H. & Lin, H. T. (1984). A Meta-analysis of Long-Term Creativity Training Programmes. *Journal of Creative Behaviour, 18(1)* 11 – 12.

Rosen, B. C. (1978). *Family Structure and achievement motivation.* American Sociology Review.

Rubenson, D. L. & Runco, M. A. (1992). The psycho-economic approach to creativity. *New Ideas Psychology, 10* 131 – 147.

Runco, A. M. (1994). *Creativity Theories and Themes: Research, Development and Practice.* Google Book Search.

Runco, M. A. & Albert, R. S. (1989). The threshold hypothesis regarding creativity and intelligence: An empirical test with gifted and nongifted children. *Creativity Child Adult Q., 11* 212 – 218.

Runco, M. A. & Charles, R. (1997). Developmental Trends in Creativity. In *Creativity Research Handbook*, ed. M. A. Runco. Cresskill, N. J.: Hampton Press.

Runco, M. A. (2004). Creativity. *Annual Review of Psychology, 55* 657 – 687.

Saha, B. (Nov., 2012). Creativity in relation to Socio-Economic Status in Secondary School Students in West Bengal. *Indian Journal of Applied Research, 2(2)* 60-61. Retrieved August 7, 2014, from www.theglobaljournals.com_ijar_file .php_val=November_ 2012_1357019382_becca_21

Sarkar, P. (1994). *A Study of Rural Children: Their Personality Pattern and Creativity.* Ph. D. Thesis (Unpublished), Kalyani University.

Sarker, A. K. (1986). *Manual of Freedom Test.* Kalyani: Dept. of Education, University of Kalyani.

Sarker, A. K. (1994). *Manual of Creativity Tests (Verbal and Non-verbal),* Kalyani: Dept. of Education, University of Kalyani.

Sarker, A. K. (1997). *Development of Family Questionnaires (I, II & III).* Kalyani: Dept. of Education, University of Kalyani.

Sarker, A. K. (1998 / 2007). *The Manual of Socio-economic Status Scale,* Kalyani: Dept. of Education, University of Kalyani.

Sarker, A. K. (Oct., 1981). Relationship of mental health and some family characteristics of middle-class school going adolescents. *Indian Education Review, 16* 1–8.

Satyanarayan, M. R. (1977). *Jejuri: Arun Kolatkar's Waste Land.* Indian Poetry in English: A Critical Assessment, Ed. V. A. Shahane and M. Sivramkrishna, Delhi: Macmillan.

Sharma, K. N. (1979 / 1985). *Dynamics of Creativity.* National Psychological Corporation, Agra.

Sharma, R. (2011). Effect of School and Home Environments on Creativity of Children. *MIER Journal of Educational Studies, Trends and Practices, 1(2).*

Siddiqi, S. (2011). A Comparative Study of Creativity among Boys and Girls of Class VII. In *Indian Educational Review, 49(2)* 5 - 14.

Simonton, D. K. (1984). *Genius, Creativity and Leadership*, Cambridge, M. A., Harvard University Press.

Simonton, D. K. (1991). Political Pathology and Societal Creativity. *Creativity Research Journal, 3* 85 - 99.

Singh, C. (1978). *Scientific Creativity Test for High School Students.* Ph. D. Thesis, Ranchi University.

Singh, R. P. (1977). Education for Creativity. *Indian Psychological Review, 14(2)* 22–25.

Singh, R. P. (1980). Divergent Thinking Abilities and Creative Personality Dimensions of Bright Adolescent Boys and Girls. A Comparative Study, *Ind. Ed. Rev., 13* 82–91.

Sinha, A. K. P. (1971). Fostering creative habits in educational system. *Indian Journal of Psychometry and Education, 2(1 & 2).*

Spearman, M. & Key, C. B. (1931). The intelligence of isolated mountain children, *Child Development, 3* 279 - 290.

Strauss, J. H. and Strauss, M. A. (1968). Family Roles and Sex Differences in Creativity of Children. In *Minneapolis J. of Marriage and Family Life, 30* 46 - 53.

Strom, R. *et al.* (Autumn, 1994). Support for Creativity in Early Adolescence. *International Journal of Sociology of the Family, 24(2)* 93–98. Retrieved August 2, 2014, from http://www.jstor.org/stable/23028656

Subotnik, R. F. & Olszewski-Kubilius, P. (1997). Restructuring special programs to reflect the distinctions between children's and adult's experiences with giftedness. *Peabody Journal of Education, 72* 101 - 116.

Sulloway, F. (1996). *Born to Rebel.* New York: Pantheon.

Taylor, C. W. (Ed.) (1972). *Climate for Creativity*, Report of the Seventh National Research Conference on Creativity. New York: John Wiley and Sons, Inc.

Tegano, D. W. & Moran, J. D. (1989). Sex differences in the original thinking of preschool and elementary school children. *Creativity Research Journal, 2* 102 - 110.

Therival, W. A. (1999). Why are eccentrics not eminently creative? *Creativity Research Journal, 12* 47 – 55.

Toby, J. (1957). The differential impact of family disorganization. *American Sociological Review.*

Tongper, R. M. (2006). *A Study on Creativity among Secondary School Students of Shillong*. Ph. D. Thesis (Unpublished), North Eastern Hill University.

Torrance, E. P. (1963). *Education and the Creative Potential.* Minneapolis University of Minnesota Press.

Torrance, E. P. (1965). *Rewarding Creative Behaviour.* Englewood Cliffs, N. J. Prentice-Hall Inc.

Torrance, E. P. (1966). *Torrance tests of creative thinking: Directions manual and sorting guide.* Princeton, N. J.: Personnel Press.

Torrance, E. P. (1969). *Guiding Creative Talent.* New Delhi: Prentice-Hall of India Pvt. Ltd.

Torrance, E. P. (1970). *Encouraging Creativity in the Class room.* Dubesque, Iowa: WmC. Brown Company Publishers.

Torrance, E. P. (1970). *Nature of Creative Talents.* In G. A. Davis and J. A. Scott, (Editors), Training Creative Thinking, New York: Holt, Rinehart and Winston, Inc., 208.

Torrance, E. P. (1977). *Discovery and Nurturance of Giftedness in the Culturally Different.* Research paper. Washington, DC: National Institute of Education.

Torrance, E. P. (Sept., 1964). Creativity in the Classroom: Respecting Children's questions and ideas. *The Instructor, 37* 129.

Torrance, E. P. and Hansesn, E. (1965). The Question asking behaviour of highly creative and less creative basic teachers identified by a paper-pencil test. *Psychological Reports, 17(5)* 815–818.

Trimurthy, S. P. (1987). A study of creative thinking ability of secondary school students in the context of some psycho-social factors. Ph. D. Thesis, SPU. In *M. B. Buch Fourth Survey of Research in Education.* 1983 - 1988.

Vandewater, E. A. & Lansford, J. E. (Oct.,1998). Influences of Family Structure and Parental Conflict on Children's Well-Being. *Family Relations,47(4)* 323–330. Retrieved August 14, 2014, from http://www.jstor.org/stable/585263

Vasasova, Z. (May 8, 2013). Creativity and its Relation to stress Perception. *Journal of Interdisciplinary Research,* 113–115. Science Daily.

Venu Gopal Rao, T. & Satyapal (2011). Socio-Economic Status, Scheduled Caste and Creativity. *International Journal of Transformations in Business Management,1(4).*

Watson, J. D. (1968). *The Double Helix.* New York: Atheneum.

Weber, M. (1947). *Essays in Sociology.* Translated by Gruth, H. H., & Wright, M. C., London: Routledge and Kegan Paul.

Wilson, R. C., Guilford, J. P. & Christensen, P. R. (1974). Relations of creative responses to working time and instructions, *Journal of Exp. Psychology,* 53 82 – 88.

Witt, L. A. & Beorkrem, M. (1989). Climate for creative productivity as a predictor of research usefulness and organizational effectiveness in an R & D organization. *Creativity Research Journal,* 2 30 – 40.

Young, D. T. & Fraser, B. J. (1994). Gender differences in science achievement. Do school effects make a difference? *Journal of Research in Science Teaching,* 31 857 – 871.

APPENDIX – A
SCORES OF ALL THE STUDENTS OF THE SAMPLE UNDER THE STUDY

SL No.	Code	Verbal Creativity			Non Verbal Creativity			Fd	SES
		Fu	*Fx*	*Or*	*Fu*	*Fx*	*Or*		
1	11102A	44	26	54	23	13	47	20	99
2	11107A	38	18	45	9	1	8	6	30
3	11110A	45	29	40	22	6	23	8	44
4	11114A	34	15	47	25	15	24	19	79
5	11115A	32	21	49	21	10	26	15	106
6	11125A	33	14	24	21	10	22	19	67
7	11126A	29	16	32	24	5	26	13	91
8	11127A	24	12	26	8	1	7	15	63
9	11131A	35	17	32	21	8	22	16	89
10	11136A	37	24	48	17	9	10	16	34
11	11143A	29	13	24	24	17	22	14	62
12	11149A	33	19	36	18	8	12	17	51
13	11158A	15	4	16	19	13	16	18	81
14	11159A	24	12	29	15	10	10	18	37
15	11160A	25	11	44	22	9	14	18	30
16	11201A	44	27	51	32	20	44	18	136
17	11202A	35	22	44	20	12	18	19	111
18	11203A	39	23	51	27	17	29	18	77
19	11204B	25	9	22	26	14	21	10	54
20	11205A	41	24	40	26	15	16	16	41
21	11205B	24	10	17	23	15	27	21	47
22	11207A	25	12	21	18	13	16	13	53
23	11209A	32	14	29	26	16	28	16	82
24	11210A	34	15	32	32	17	30	11	140
25	11217A	28	16	24	21	11	24	12	75
26	11218A	32	15	29	27	11	31	9	75
27	11220B	30	14	24	20	10	15	12	75
28	11222A	24	4	14	32	18	33	14	92
29	11223B	17	3	7	26	18	25	8	50
30	11224B	35	17	39	24	14	22	19	66
31	11226B	26	6	18	19	6	14	15	92
32	11228A	27	12	32	27	15	24	9	120
33	11237A	18	3	12	17	11	11	16	108
34	11239A	31	13	29	19	10	20	15	89
35	11243A	31	12	36	19	12	24	18	85
36	11244A	20	6	19	24	12	22	17	46
37	11254A	19	5	13	19	12	17	12	97

Appendix Contd...

SL No.	*Code*	*Verbal Creativity*			*Non Verbal Creativity*			*Fd*	*SES*
		Fu	*Fx*	*Or*	*Fu*	*Fx*	*Or*		
-	-	-	-	-	-	-	-	-	-
-	-	-	-	-	-	-	-	-	-
356	22601B	33	22	45	44	24	37	18	45
357	22604B	24	13	32	33	18	30	7	25
358	22607B	34	20	40	21	12	14	16	89
359	22611B	34	14	33	28	11	23	12	111
360	22612B	28	19	39	19	11	19	13	100
361	22615B	42	27	46	33	9	20	15	88
362	22621B	28	12	27	29	19	30	18	110
363	22622B	28	13	30	26	17	27	24	71
364	22622B	26	17	27	28	13	33	24	71
365	22623A	41	27	46	33	18	40	9	89
366	22625A	42	28	43	35	24	34	11	44
367	22627A	32	20	33	37	22	40	11	101
368	22629A	29	16	38	37	14	46	17	77
369	22630B	32	19	35	34	15	24	16	45
370	22630B	34	15	24	32	19	43	16	45
371	22651A	37	21	40	14	6	14	15	98
372	22655A	27	12	32	30	16	26	19	80

Notations used

Fu = Fluency, Fx = Flexibility, Or = Originality, Fd = Freedom, SES = Socio-economic Status of the family.

The above table contained the data of Creativity (verbal and non-verbal) in the dimensions of Fluency, Flexibility and Originality along with Freedom, Socio-economic Status of 372 students out of which 179 students were boys and 193 students were girls of both class VIII and class IX of different schools.

APPENDIX – B

DATA CONVERTED INTO T-SCORES

CODE	*FU_V C_T*	*FX_V C_T*	*OR_V C_T*	*FU_N VC_T*	*FX_N VC_T*	*OR_N VC_T*	*FU_T_ TOT*	*FX_T_ TOT*	*OR_T_ TOT*	*FD*	*SES*
11102A	64.77	66.83	70.21	44.2	46.44	69.77	108.97	113.27	139.97	20	99
11107A	58.01	54.71	62.15	24.56	23.57	31.86	82.57	78.28	94.01	6	30
11110A	65.89	71.38	57.67	42.8	33.1	46.44	108.69	104.47	104.11	8	44
11114A	53.51	50.17	63.94	47.01	50.25	47.41	100.52	100.41	111.35	19	79
11115A	51.26	59.26	65.73	41.4	40.72	49.36	92.66	99.98	115.09	15	106
11125A	52.39	48.65	43.34	41.4	40.72	45.47	93.78	89.37	88.81	19	67
11126A	47.88	51.68	50.5	45.61	31.19	49.36	93.49	82.87	99.86	13	91
11127A	42.26	45.62	45.13	23.15	23.57	30.89	65.41	69.19	76.02	15	63
11131A	54.64	53.2	50.5	41.4	36.91	45.47	96.03	90.11	95.97	16	89
11136A	56.89	63.8	64.83	35.78	38.81	33.81	92.67	102.62	98.64	16	34
11143A	47.88	47.14	43.34	45.61	54.06	45.47	93.49	101.2	88.81	14	62
11149A	52.39	56.23	54.08	37.19	36.91	35.75	89.57	93.14	89.84	17	51
11158A	32.13	33.5	36.17	38.59	46.44	39.64	70.72	79.94	75.81	18	81
11159A	42.26	45.62	47.81	32.98	40.72	33.81	75.23	86.34	81.62	18	37
11160A	43.38	44.11	61.25	42.8	38.81	37.7	86.18	82.92	98.95	18	30
11201A	64.77	68.35	67.52	56.83	59.78	66.85	121.6	128.12	134.37	18	136
11202A	54.64	60.77	61.25	39.99	44.53	41.58	94.63	105.3	102.83	19	111
11203A	59.14	62.29	67.52	49.82	54.06	52.27	108.96	116.34	119.79	18	77
11204B	43.38	41.08	41.55	48.41	48.34	44.5	91.8	89.42	86.04	10	54
11205A	61.39	63.8	57.67	48.41	50.25	39.64	109.8	114.05	97.31	16	41

-	-	-	-	-	-	-	-	-	-	-	-
-	-	-	-	-	-	-	-	-	-	-	-
22622B	42.17	50.85	44.7	52.87	49.05	56.14	95.04	99.9	100.83	24	71
22623A	60.58	65.32	59.71	60.28	59.62	62.96	120.86	124.94	122.68	9	89
22625A	61.81	66.77	57.34	63.24	72.3	57.11	125.05	139.07	114.45	11	44
22627A	49.53	55.19	49.44	66.2	68.07	62.96	115.73	123.27	112.4	11	101
22629A	45.85	49.41	53.39	66.2	51.16	68.82	112.05	100.57	122.21	17	77
22630B	49.53	53.75	51.02	61.76	53.28	47.36	111.29	107.02	98.38	16	45
22630B	51.99	47.96	42.33	58.79	61.73	65.89	110.78	109.69	108.22	16	45
22651A	55.67	56.64	54.97	32.14	34.25	37.6	87.82	90.89	92.57	15	98
22655A	43.4	43.62	48.65	55.83	55.39	49.31	99.23	99.01	97.96	19	80

Notations Used:

FU = Fluency

FX = Flexibility

OR = Originality

VC = Verbal Creativity

NVC = Non-Verbal Creativity

T = After converted in T-score

T_TOT = Total after converted in T-scores